From Budapest to Paris (1936–1957)

From Budapest to Paris (1936–1957)

An Autobiography

MIKLOS VETO

foreword by Peter Ochs

translated by Rajat D. Acharya

RESOURCE *Publications* • Eugene, Oregon

FROM BUDAPEST TO PARIS (1936–1957)
An Autobiography

Resource Publications
An Imprint of Wipf and Stock Publishers
199 W. 8th Ave., Suite 3
Eugene, OR 97401

www.wipfandstock.com

PAPERBACK ISBN: 978-1-5326-6822-7
HARDCOVER ISBN: 978-1-5326-6823-4
EBOOK ISBN: 978-1-5326-6824-1

Manufactured in the U.S.A. 06/19/20

Contents

Foreword

THIS WONDROUS BOOK IS the biographical, philosophic, and theological self-reflection of a singularly devout Catholic who remains deeply attached to his Jewish and his Hungarian identities, however much they were seared by his youthful passage through some of the darkest years of human history, 1936—1957. What we see on each page of this narrative depends upon the fears, hopes, and imaginings we bring with us individually. We may see the darkness of unmitigated human sin, the worldly consequences of political and ideological totalitarianism, the Nazi Holocaust, anti-Semitism, self-serving nationalist racism, the utter brutality of international and nationalist Soviet and Hungarian Communism, the unimaginable efforts of humans to remove not only the lives but also the dignity and also the divine image that shows its face in other humans. We may see the redeeming light of a human being's passionate relation to God: glimpsed, for example, through the narrative of how a young, assimilated Hungarian Jew, surrounded by this darkness since the age of four or five, is sheltered by Catholic-Jewish relatives in Budapest; is carried—by his own intellect, the resources of libraries, and the care of a few friends, relatives and teachers— to other realms of vision and apperception; and is embraced, in his teenage years, by an all embracing and immovable faith in the one he calls "the Lord Jesus Christ." Or, if privileged to have been his student or to have read his profound and extensive writings, we may rejoin something familiar (the process of his great mind at work) as it uncovers something unfamiliar: Veto's philosophic, religious, and spiritual self-examination.

As I read Veto's narrating what he experienced during the years of Holocaust, of the Hungarian revolution, and of migrations in search of a place to live and teach, I picture the sociopolitical environments as I have pictured them through many histories of the mid to late 20th century. As I read Veto's narrating religious and spiritual experiences, I visualize what I have seen through the books of Catholic mysticism we studied in his undergraduate classes. But when I read his theo-philosophic self-reflections, I no longer have eyes to see; I am stimulated to imagine conceptual forms and relations I had not previously imagined in this particular way. I conclude with a sample of such forms and relations, trusting that each reader would imagine these differently.

The Self Unified in God's Light. Veto writes that human life is a totality of which each part counts, but certain moments count more than the others. He writes that the first 20 years of his life prefigure everything that follows, a claim that is consistent with his *metaphysics of the child*. But prefiguration implies some form of narrative unity, and it is difficult to imagine what could possibly bring unity to the shockingly disparate and disruptive events of his early life. Veto offers a clue in his concluding pages: "I received the Faith suddenly, without any preparation, in a single instant, unnuanced, without interior or exterior relation. And I essentially continue to 'have' it in this foundational manner." The discontinuities within this life of faith "attest, in their fragmentary, imperfect manner, to the movement toward a term, a term which is as much already attained as it is remaining to be attained." This faith is thus "a principle of life" that reaches dynamically into and across a life's disparate stages, binding them into a unity with Him that is fully realized only in the present and coming life with Him.

Identities: Veto's autobiography narrates the dynamic relations among three of his unities of self: what he calls his familial, his Hungarian, and his Jewish identities. Narrating dramatic events in each stage of his younger years, Veto is at the same time writing the story of each of these identities. He writes with a flowing pen, as if the writing were his activity of remembering as much and as rapidly as he could, re-opening images that might have arisen out of this funny childhood encounter with Aunty Irén, or that time spent in the kitchen with beloved Grandma (center of childhood), and as if the remembering were his keys to unlocking more than memory. I imagine he was unlocking anamnesis as understood both by Plato, recollecting the divine work that preceded his birth, and by the Church, recollecting the sacrifice and the redemption of Christ. If so, the autobiography is also an activity of *lending* unity to his diverse lives as he brings those lives to consciousness and consecrates them to the One with whom, alone, they are one.

Darkness and Light. Remembering how the Biblical narrative traces the life of Israel and the life of Jesus Christ through this darkened world, I read Veto's autobiography as narrating the movement of divine light as if it were refracted through the dark prism of those years, 1936–1957, and projected onto the pages of a book. It is no idealized narrative. He received the dogmas of his faith "like a stone—or rather like a bomb—fallen from on high. [The faith] came from elsewhere to throw itself into an emptiness, a void. It filled this void, but, strangely, the void remains. . . ." We should not, however, be too quick read this psychologically. "This void corresponds, so to speak, with the coming of Christ, Who, while having taken flesh, remains in the heart of the Father." As a rabbinic Jew, I will not presume to know what Veto means. But I will report what I am led to imagine.

Veto writes that all his "identities are gathered and united in the Catholic identity, the force, the power, which accomplishes and articulates their synthesis." But he receives this faith as *philosopher* as well as devotee, and his instruments of self-examination are as much of the intellect as of the heart. As theo-philosopher, he contemplates the *form* of his relation to God as well as the matter and content. This form, he writes, is of the Trinity, for God is a person, "and philosophy shows and demonstrates that one is not a person but with another person." The relation of person-to-person is love, and the activity of that love is not confined to any person but goes-toward yet another: "as in the Creation. . ., then in the Incarnation. . . in order to save this created world fallen into sin." I imagine that, for Veto, just as His creating the world is movement into the void, so is His saving work.

Peter Ochs
(college student of Miklos Veto's, 1967–1971; life-long student since then)

Translator's Preface

THE WORK THAT I have translated is a searching reflection by one of the important philosophers of our time upon his own life. Yet its search has at least three different dimensions. Firstly, and most obviously, the author has sought to reflect the critical events that have oriented and formed his life. Secondly, from beneath and between these events, there is reflected his own search for a more profound understanding of his own identity. But, thirdly, insofar as he has chosen to share this search, its reflection casts a certain brilliant luminosity upon the reader. This is the manner in which I have profited from what the author has shared. And, it is for this reason that I have wished to share it with the Anglophone world.

The original French text resembles an ornate tapestry that depicts the complicated journey of a life, or rather, its several journeys. Most obvious is the physical one of geographic displacement: from Budapest to Paris. Hence, it has been chosen as the title of this book. However, this title serves as the synecdochic cover for the other journeys, some of which it would be useful to name: from the fragmentation of one family to the flourishing of another; from a disinterested illiteracy and delayed schooling to a busy academic life of letters; from being violently oppressed and persecuted in one country to being appreciated in many countries; and, of course, from a self-confessed atheism to a fervent Catholicism. I hope that my translation, presently before the reader, approximates to doing the journeys of this life some justice, or at least no injustice.

R. D. ACHARYA
Le Saulchoir
Paris, France
February 20, 2019

Author's Preface

EACH MOMENT OF THE entire human life counts. But of such moments, some count more than others. Life has epochs, and the first of them—the first twenty years—has perhaps more import than those that follow. These early years, from unconscious origins to physical and intellectual blossoming, found and, in a certain manner, prefigure those which follow. To be sure, each day brings the new, but the new is rooted in that which precedes it. The last sixty years of my life are like a late blossoming. They have not all gone smoothly, but even disruptions are ultimately for appreciation and understanding, based on the roots, the origins: birth before the Second World War into a Jewish family in Hungary; the deportations; the death of my parents; adoption by my aunt and uncle; my studies at a grand high school in Budapest; my fervent reading of history and poetry; and two final determining factors: the religious experience, having taken place one day in February 1954, which turned me from a young atheist-agnostic into a fervent Catholic; and, my participation in the Revolution of 1956, which led to my flight west.

The events of these twenty years are described in the three chapters that follow. The postface continues with the sixty years that have passed since my arrival in France. First to have taken place were my studies at the Sorbonne and then at Oxford, my marriage to Odile and our twelve years in America, the birth of our children and university postings. Subsequently, we experienced an African interlude, with four years in Abidjan. Finally, we returned to France where I continued teaching in universities and then began my retirement. All of this has been accompanied, penetrated, and illuminated by philosophical creativity, resulting with a long suite of books and articles. The postface thus presents, in an abridged fashion, such moments and events of my life. And these pages are an attempt to discern and express the personal continuities that constitute its armature. They are intended to show how my origins have led me to become that which I am. They are intended to make known the philosopher, the husband to his wife of fifty-six years, the father of three children, and the fervent Catholic.

Before commencing the account, gratitude is due. To my wife who, as usual, has read everything, but this time with a particularly keen interest for the content. To my friend Jean-François de Raymond, who has carefully read and annotated the original version, almost three times longer than the little book that has come out of it. To Julie Lachance who, with an infallible sense of the Quebecian French, has read and weighed each word and comma of the French original. Finally, I intend to express my gratitude to Bruno Péquignot for two decades of collaboration, which resulted with the publication of some twenty works by my hand in the collection managed by him.

Miklós Vető

1

Childhood: From Felcsút to Budapest

I WAS BORN ON August 22, 1936, in Budapest. My parents lived in Felcsút, in the county of Fejér, roughly forty kilometers from Budapest. That was quite far in those days, especially if one didn't have a car, which was the case for us. We had a property of some three hundred and fifty hectares, and a quartz sand mine (indispensable for Hungarian metallurgy), however my family was very traditional, so were content with horse-drawn carriage. In fact, we had six of them, one of which was completely black and grandiose, having originally belonged to the archduke Joseph of Habsburg, who lived three kilometers away from us. We had one coach driver for the week, but we had another for Sundays—this one with a magnificent moustache. When he died, one of his friends lamented over the tragic event by saying: "It is a pity that this moustache will henceforth find itself in the tomb."

The family had two houses. One of them was larger, inhabited by my widowed grandmother, one of my aunts who was also widowed, a single cousin, and another cousin who was not completely normal. That one, Iluci (Ilona), collected postage stamps, read books for little girls, and was mocked by the maids who told her that they would arrange a marriage for her . . . The larger house, which the peasants called the "big castle," had nine main rooms; the "little castle," four. I lived in this smaller house with my parents and my little brother, István, two years my junior. The two houses were encircled by gardens of flowers, fruit trees, and bushes. I particularly loved the lilacs, violet or white. There was also an immense hazel tree, which stands to this day. In the spring, we waited for the first flowers to blossom: the snowdrops, then the violets. The two houses were roughly fifty meters from the main street of Felcsút. (Felcsút had two streets.) One entered via a bridge which crossed a ditch. On each side, there was an enormous piece of carved rock, which made part of a roman sarcophagus: the tomb of a woman that had been found in the fields of our property. My grandfather, a patriotic and generous citizen, donated jewels and utensils contained within the tomb to the county museum, saving nothing for the family but two heavy bronze arrows. The donation had taken place decades before my birth, but I'd have preferred it remain with my grandfather . . .

Life in Felcsút was antediluvian, feudal. The village had two landowners: the Kozmas, and us. The Kozma family castle is today called, after the historical hero of Hungarian football, the Ferenc Puskás Academy of Sport.[1] The Kozmas lived in Budapest, and they had some fifty hectares more than us. I tried to relativize this truth by also counting as our land the further three hundred hectares of another property that belonged to the son-in-law of my grandfather. This land had been sold before the Great War, but I continued to include them in our property . . . Felcsút had some seventeen hundred inhabitants, essentially peasants, among whom many agricultural workers lived in very great poverty. I of course played with the peasant children, but these youngsters of my own age, to whom I spoke quite casually, only spoke with respectful formality to me. They had barely any toys, and one day I received a splendid gift, a magnificent tricycle, which was to replace another, an antique, that was not itself in bad condition. All of a sudden, I had a surge of generosity: I offered the new tricycle to one of the small peasant children, who left with it, mad with joy. But I began to have regrets, and went to my mother telling her that, deep down, that little peasant had really no need of a brand-new tricycle. "Why don't you ask him to return it in exchange for the old one?" (That one which had been relegated to the granary amidst boxes, suitcases, bags, broken rocking chairs, and damaged umbrellas.) But my mother didn't budge: "You have given him your tricycle; you're not going to take it back from him." There was nothing to be done, and I was left rather somber.

We had a housemaid and a nursemaid. In fact, I began with the nursemaid because Mama had no more milk, and so I had a milk brother. I lost track of him, but at the defeat of the Revolution of '56, in which he was a very active participant, he was arrested and in danger of being sentenced

1. The Prime Minister, Viktor Orbán, an inhabitant of the town, until only recently played in the Felcsút football team.

to capital punishment. My (adoptive) father, a lawyer, defended him, and saved his head . . . I believe he was freed after six years in prison, during the great amnesty from '63 to '64 . . . The family used to have lunch with the children. There was a big table for the parents and a small one for the boys, and I remember that we always had a glass of water with a few drops of wine, the product of our property. I was a small boy, rather lively, and when I misbehaved, I was sent to the corner behind a big ceramic stove. But I had quite comfortably settled into the spot. I had a little stool, a hammer, and a kind of small chisel, and each time that I was relegated behind the stove, I continued to bore a hole in the wall. When the maid saw what I had done, she said to me: "You see, tonight the mice will climb up from the cellar through this hole." I didn't close my eyes throughout that entire night.[2]

The "castles" were situated very close to the farm buildings: barns for horses, cows, sheep, and pigs. We always had fresh milk. One day, we were taken to see newborn baby lambs, and we were given one each. I remember that István and I had a competition to see which of these two lambs, his or mine, would have its horns first. I finally won this little brotherly contest. But I also remember that, beside the barn for the cows, there was an enormous basin for the manure, and that, during the winter, all of it was frozen over. Now, István had a wet nurse, and the farm boys decided to play a little trick on this girl from Budapest. They said to her: "Go through there, Miss. Forward . . ." They were directing her to walk atop the basin of manure, frozen over by the cold. All of a sudden, the sheet of ice shattered, and she found herself up to her knees in dung. She climbed out of it, screaming, only to realize that she had lost one of her shoes. She returned to find it. I can still see myself laughing while leaning on the wall of the barn. It is perhaps the first memory of my life, and the other refers to a car. Uncle Jenő, a deputy and one of the more celebrated lawyers in Hungary, had a car and chauffeur. The car was parked on the main street, and I posed questions to the chauffeur about its operation. I think that was the first and last time that I was interested in a car.

2. Another of my achievements: One day, we were invited to a lunch. I went onto all fours under the table, and with a small pair of scissors, I carefully cut the pants of the guests, who were themselves engaged in a lively conversation . . . When I was mischievous, mainly at night, when I didn't want to leave my grandmother's house, Julis, one of the maids, used to wrap me in the "grey coat" (an old overcoat having belonged to my great grandfather), and no matter how much I struggled, I was inevitably transported to the "little castle." And I was equally far from being exemplary toward outside people. For example, I was routinely taken to the hairdresser, but I used to scream and gesticulate so much that he ended up not wanting me anymore. It came to the point that when he caught sight of our carriage, he would climb down the awning of his boutique and flee through his garden.

As I said, we had no car, so when Grandma went to Budapest, accompanied by one of the maids, she was driven in a taxi. The taxi came from Bicske, a small town of six thousand inhabitants, five kilometers from Felcsút. The chauffeur arrived and, to prepare himself for the rigor of the voyage (almost forty kilometers), he swallowed an omelet made with six eggs.

This memory prompts me to speak of Grandma. She was the center of my life as a child. I loved her with all my heart, so much that I was brought to tears while thinking of her sixty years after her death. I was the second last of her grandchildren—the eldest, the poor Iluci, was twenty-four years my senior—but I think that I was truly her favorite. I telephoned her each morning, that is, until the young lady who was the operator in the village received instructions not to connect my communications. Every morning, we, István and I, went to see Grandma. She would be in the kitchen, preparing dishes and directing the two young maids. At our arrival, she steered us toward the grand dining room, one of the rooms kept shut practically all the time. (Everyday life after all only took place in three or four of the nine rooms that the house comprised.) Therein, we received chocolate, currants, and almonds. The slabs of chocolate seemed immense to me; I never again found the same. I used to return in the afternoon to pass close to two hours at Grandma's house, and it was Aunty Juliska (Julie), a first cousin of my father, who looked after me. She used to tell me stories, mainly of her cat. It was pure pleasure, trance-like. It was necessary that she narrated these to me without interruption. And if she stopped to cough, I would put my hand on her mouth to prevent anything other than words of the story from coming out of it. Aunty Julie was an old girl, adorable, intelligent, and peculiar. Her principal interests were astronomy, equitation, and the fabrication of artificial flowers. Immediately after the war, she received a parcel from the United States with a note mentioning that she should pay customs fees. Having arrived at the customs office, she began to protest: the fees demanded of her were not high enough. The customs officer, thinking that she was crazy, simply sent her walking.

All of this was the perfect life of a child, a paradise in which all was harmonious. My parents lived in love. As for my little brother, I often squabbled with him, but that wasn't of any consequence. It's true that I was the dominating older brother. I did not let him speak, and he ended up stammering for a while. When, after the war, we were separated, I missed him terribly, and I felt remorse, sentiments of culpability for having mistreated him. But, beyond my parents and baby brother, the center of this paradise, and its principal source, was my grandmother. She was born Weisz (our paternal family was also called Weisz), 1869, in Zombor, a small town of the Bácska ("Sombor" in the Serbian Voïvodina of today). It was her paternal great grandfather, Salamon Weisz, who had emigrated from Galicia to Hungary in 1806. Galicia, Western Ukraine today, like Hungary, belonged to the Habsburg Empire. It consisted of countries of different juridical status, but there were no borders to separate them. My grandmother never spoke of Salamon Weisz. On the other hand, she recounted to me a story concerning another great grandpa. Abraham Lederer was born in 1785 and was, at the age of ninety-six years, in good health. Having built a new wooden fence around his house, he declared: "I will keep it for another decade." But this poor man had the habit of napping after lunch, just beside the fireplace. And one day, in his sleep, he fell into the fire, suffering burns, and dying the following day in terrible pain. It's a very sad story, but also one of those properly historical stories that connect you almost physically to the past. I knew my grandmother well, and she knew someone who was born before the French Revolution.

The paternal grandfather of Grandma, József Weisz, was a primary school teacher in the Jewish community of Zombor. He was enlisted in the army during the Hungarian Revolution of 1848–1849. He participated in twenty-two battles, and his wife, with their children, followed him in a kind of covered car, which he generally entered for lunch . . . After the defeat of the Revolution, in danger of being arrested, he had to hide himself for a while.[3] His portrait and a kind of attestation to his services as a revolutionary fighter are suspended on the wall of my brother's house. From the year 1870, Hungary experienced an immense economic development, and the Jews, having just come out of the ghetto, took part in it with dazzling success. Grandma's father, Zsigmond Weisz, had relocated to Budapest and became a rich wheat merchant. Grandma completed her education in Budapest. She was a cultivated woman who read novels in German and French. In 1890, she married a landowner from Felcsút who was also called Zsigmond Weisz. I didn't know this grandfather. He died of a heart attack in 1925, when he was sixty-eight years old.

Grandma was the eldest of five. She had two sisters: Flora, who died at forty-two years from the Spanish flu, and Erzsóka (Elisabeth). Erzsóka was the sole survivor among those brothers and sisters of my grandmother whom I knew. She died in the December of 1956, two months before my flight west. For me, she was one of the closer members of the family, even though I don't remember in my entire life ever having exchanged more than a few words with her, each one utterly insignificant. Aunty Erzsóka had no children, but she had dogs and a famous husband. Uncle Jenő, the owner of the car I admired in Felcsút, was a great criminal lawyer who pleaded in

3. See p. 58.

political trials. One, for example, was of Hungarian aristocrats who counterfeited millions of francs in order to lower the value of the French currency, hated because of the Treaty of Trianon, a peace treaty that mutilated Hungary by severing almost three quarters of its territory. To defend Prince Windischgraetz and his accomplices, Jenő Gal spoke for three consecutive days, twelve hours per day! As a law student, Uncle Jenő won the Canon Law Grand Prize at the University of Budapest. The Dean called him into his office to say to him: "Young man, you are a brilliant subject. You have before you a dazzling career, but it is for that reason that you must be baptized." The young man thanked the Dean for his benevolence, but refused. Although, forty years later, during legislative elections in a district with many Protestants, he was seen going to the Holy Table . . . He was elected and remained deputy until his death in 1940. Aunty Erzsóka was petite, but she wore in her hair, from time to time, magnificent ostrich feathers, which made her appear taller. The Gals had a vast apartment on Saint-Stephen Boulevard, beside an important theatre. Of the apartment's six rooms, five looked out onto the street. The smallest overlooked the courtyard. And that was the room in which they lived, while the big rooms, well-furnished, remained closed. They obviously also had an immense bathroom, but to avoid sullying it, Uncle Jenő had to use the local public showers . . . Aunty Erzsóka had one passion: the kitchen. The walls of her office were covered in jars of apricot jam of decreasing size. Her preparation of pickles in vinegar, with dill and green bell pepper or finely chopped cabbage, were universally recognized. Having no children, she poured her affection upon one of her nieces, Manci (the diminutive of Madeleine). One day, she told this niece to sit down in front of her. "Manci," she asked, "tell me the truth. Which *Eingeschlagenes* (a sumptuous Jewish cake) is better, the one made by my sister Ilona, or mine?" Manci had realized what was at stake, clearly grasping the danger. A sense of honor and diplomacy were at war in her soul. But, at last, she said with a feeble voice: "Aunty Erzsóka, your *Eingeschlagenes* is excellent, but the one made by Aunty Ilona is still better." "This, Manci,"—the sentence fell—"I will not pardon of you, not even on my deathbed."

The three brothers of Grandma were artists. The eldest, Jenő, was a composer, and his operas and operettas continued to be played even fifty years after his death. Sandor, the painter, lived in Paris. But when the War erupted in 1914, he immediately returned to enlist. He fell some weeks later in Bucovina on the Russian front. One of his sceneries, a countryside, is currently in my brother's apartment. The third and youngest of the brothers, József, was an orchestral conductor, but above all the parasite of the family. When his parents departed for Nice during Christmas, leaving József in their apartment, the young Manci advised her grandfather: "You should lock your safe." "Lock it? For what danger? You're not going to suspect *my* son . . ." On their return, they discovered the safe empty . . . The parents ended up no longer supporting József's escapades and sent him with a *one-way* boat ticket to New York. He never again got back in touch. István and I, young children, had fantasies of the millions of dollars that he was going to leave us. He died in '44 as the orchestral conductor of the Waldorf Astoria Hotel, but without leaving us a penny. In fact, his friends had to pay for his funeral.

The paradise that was our life in Felcsút suffered its first rupture on May 14, 1941. During the previous night, my father had opened up his veins, and was found dead in the morning. He had come to our bedroom in the evening and, as usual, kissed us in our beds. In fact, I seem to remember him being even more affectionate than usual. But the following day, the house was in a strange state. Half of it was closed off from the children, and my uncle, a doctor, the husband of the older sister of Mama, had arrived with his car from Budapest. We were not told that our father was dead, but that he had gone to be treated in a sanatorium.[4] Almost ten months passed before I finally learnt the truth. At that point, I fainted.[5] I only ever fainted once thereafter, when I learnt that my adoptive father had returned from deportation. I loved my father passionately. He placed me, from time to time, in front of himself when he roamed his lands on horseback. Among my more detailed memories of him, perhaps the last was of the time we went together on a small journey to a grain shop in Bicske. He told me to choose seeds that are to grow in a patch of land that he was going to give to me. Not knowing what to choose, he "suggested" to me that we buy sugar beet seeds, which we in fact sowed the day after. I subsequently went each day to see whether the beets had grown. I was quite disappointed by the delay, the endless wait, but I had never wanted to continue the work of my father anyway. The land never really interested me.

My father was a passionate patriot. At eighteen years, he enlisted in the White Army of Horthy; one could count with one's fingers the Jewish officers in these battalions! He was going to save the life of a peasant of Felcsút, the leader of the village during the Commune of 1919, when the militia of

4. I have a strange memory of the day that followed the death of my father: I saw him coming to see us in our room, without saying anything. But, at that time, he had not been alive for at least ten hours.

5. Two years later, when I was about to learn of the death of my grandmother, my mother, fearing my reaction, stammered something. I said to her: "Do not tell me that she's gone to a sanatorium . . ." During a recent retreat in Cacouna, Quebec, I understood that this loss of consciousness was a defense reaction to "shield" me, so to speak, against great trials in my life.

the White Army wanted to execute him. The Red Terror had given way to the White Terror . . . Still during the Commune, the Communists detained, in his neighboring castle in Alcsút, Archduke Joseph, who was formally the commander of the Austro-Hungarian Army on the Italian front. The Communists wanted to starve him, but my father and my grandfather succeeded in having food supplies sent to him. When, twenty years later, the first anti-Jewish laws were voted, my father asked for intervention by the archduke to help the family. The archduke, who was at that time the president of the High Chamber of the Parliament, was circumvented. He had, he said, no influence over anything at all . . . My father was still going to participate as an officer in the liberation of Ruszinszkó, the small Subcarpathian territory that had always belonged to Hungary but was attributed to Czechoslovakia by the Treaty of Trianon. I remember quite vaguely that upon his return in September 1939, he brought back for us some kind of small neckties, fashioned out of glass beads. Less than two years later, he was taken by depression, sadly present in some members of the family, which was surely triggered by dark predictions concerning the situation of the Jews. This depression drove him to suicide.

Three days later, István and I were baptized at a church in Budapest. The adults wanted to save us from the coming persecutions. István has no memory of that ceremony, but I recall that he struggled when the holy water washed over his head. The priest declared—whether humorously, there is question—that he must be possessed by the devil. For someone who was not even three years old, that must have been a feat . . . My grandmother, floored by the death of her youngest son, was never going to learn that we had been baptized. She was the only member of the family who looked positively upon being Jewish. She was, to be sure, not really practicing. (On Saturdays, we had *solet*, a Jewish bean dish, with . . . smoked ham . . .[6]) But she thought of herself as Jewish, and she wanted at least the adults to fast on the day of Yom Kippur. Apart from her, the family was completely estranged from the Jewish faith. I remember both of my aunts being astonished to learn that a relative by marriage, "a man yet young," frequented the synagogue! In 1898, my grandfather Hungarianized his name from Weisz to Vető (Sower of Seed), but he barely had any attraction for his religion from birth. If he had not been baptized, according to the reading of my adoptive father, it was likely due to pride: I am "fine" the way I am . . . Undoubtedly, tolerance had a limit: When my adoptive father was about to marry his second wife, a Christian—a "goy"—she, who was about to become my adoptive mother,

6. See p. 89.

was not received by her mother-in-law for two years.[7] It is true, however, that Grandma had thenceforth affectionately taken her in. Grandpa was a cultivated man with a beautiful library, and in his youth he even published, at his own expense, two small volumes of (very bad) poetry. He was the vice-president of the liberal party of the county, the party in power in Budapest. He had received letters of praise from Ottokár Prohászka, Bishop of Székesfehérvár, the most important writer and Christian philosopher in Hungary of his time.

During the Great War, Russian prisoners of war were settled into buildings on the property. They were, I believe, mainly those who were wounded, because the authorities had opened a military hospital in these buildings. My grandmother and my two aunts, Florence and Irén, had received training to be nurses, and were going to be honored as such. Grandma always told me that the Russian prisoners of war were, in that hospital, not treated differently to the Hungarian soldiers.

After the death of my father, my mother courageously yoked herself to the task of taking over the direction of the property. She also wandered the land on horseback, but she quickly recognized that she would be unable to continue this work alone. She took on, therefore, stewards, three successively, I believe, who were not very competent. My only memory of the last of them was that he was a hunter, like my father, and had one time brought back a magnificent pheasant, which had the colors of blue and gold. My mother had to be quite solitary at Felcsút. After all, the "society" was reduced to a minimum: the parish priest, the Calvinist pastor, and the village doctor—those who at that time were the regulars in my grandfather's weekly card games. As for the peasants, our relationship with them was of feudal order, but marked by goodwill. My father was frowned upon by most of the other landowners in the county because he paid his laborers better than the other employers, and it was also known that he greeted each one of his employees before there was even time for them to remove their hats. As for my grandmother, her house served as an establishment of formation for a great number of girls in the village who were successively her maids. She taught them how to keep a house, and watched over them. However, many of these young girls, despite their rooms being locked by key during the night, managed to conceive a child before marriage . . . Grandma followed the lives of these young women, and gave them wedding presents. We were particularly close to some peasant families, including the Bakonyis. Julis (Julia) Bakonyi, who died a nonagenarian in 2014, was her last maid;

7. According to family tradition, my grandmother one day received an open postcard by one of her sisters-in-law: "One misfortune after another. One of the steers on my husband's property has broken its leg and my son has just married a Christian . . ."

Grandma died in her arms. Old man Bakonyi had such a fidelity to our family that, under the Communist Regime, he refused to enter into the Hungarian version of the kolkhoz. He was sanctioned and denied his retirement payment. Of course, when we came to learn of his situation in 1976, with a Western income, it was easy for us to compensate him for what he had lost. When the persecutions began, my family gathered the women's jewels. Half were entrusted to an amicable medical doctor, who was, supposedly, going to hide them underground. The other half were put into the hands of the Bakonyi family. The doctor "lost" some of the diamonds. Those confided to the farmer were all returned to us after the war by him!

I should have begun primary school in '42, but it was inconceivable that I have my classes among peasant children in the school of the village. The solution would have been for me to leave for Budapest, but we wanted to spare my grandmother, for she had been profoundly affected by the death of my father. So, a woman of a certain age had been recruited to teach me how to read and write. I however disappointed the family because I had no desire to begin to read. It was not until during the summer of '43 when, glued to the bed by a mild fever, I was so bored that, in my desperation, I began to read a book that recounted the adventures of Muki and Bubu—a monkey and an elephant who had come from their native Congo to the Budapest zoo. The book had ninety pages, and I finished it in three days. Thereafter, things accelerated, such that at around my seventh birthday I was able to read the six large volumes of the illustrated history of the world.

We left Felcsút in the month of June, '43. When it was announced to me that we were henceforth going to live in Budapest, I didn't want to accept it. My heart was split in two, and all had collapsed. We had to abandon our house, because at that time the land that belonged to Jews could be confiscated and assigned to those in service of the Horthy regime. In principle, only some rooms of Grandma's house were considered confiscable property, but, quite rapidly, she ended up being evicted from the home in which she had lived for fifty-three years. The family found her a rentable villa in a very pleasant quarter of Budapest. She was going to die six months later, but she had the greatest joy to learn, on the day before her death, that my (adoptive) father, being a lawyer, succeeded to convince the Supreme Court of the illegality of her eviction, and that her house was to be returned to the family. Of course, the juridical decision did not have any actual consequence. This is fortunate, because if the family was found in Felcsút during the April of '44, it would have suffered the same fate as the Jews living outside Budapest—almost all of them were going to be deported to Auschwitz. The Jews of Felcsút were gassed. Of them, only Grandma's seamstress and the two youngest of the watchmaker's ten children were the exceptions who would return.

2

From Childhood to Adolescence

Mama, my brother, and I were welcomed into the house of my maternal grandmother, who had herself just become a widow. My maternal grandfather, Sandor Aczél, was an agreeable man, a cultivated man, and a man submissive to his wife. Fifty-five years after his death, a neighbor while grinning mightily said of him: "He was a very 'sweet [*doux*]' man . . ."[1] Grandpa had retired as the director of a bank agency. He played chess with friends in the park, read a lot, and, toward his seventy-fifth birthday, learnt his seventh foreign language (Spanish). He also prepared their housekeeper's natural son for his high school exams. We called her [this housekeeper] Aunty Teri (Theresa) (because, if Aristotle was able to remark that young children call every adult man "father" and woman "mother," in Hungary, as in most of Central Europe, one calls every older man and woman "uncle" and "aunt"). Aunty Teri often brought us, by way of the little cogwheel train that departed from just opposite our building, into the hills of Budapest to search for crystals. And she was herself overjoyed when she could drive us to the Lilliput Theatre,[2] where dwarves played simple pieces for what was essentially a juvenile audience. Another image that returns to me is of the time she drove us to the house of one of her friends, the maid

1. [Trans.] "*Doux*" can mean "sweet," but also "soft."

2. Lilliput was the name of the land of the little people in Jonathan Swift's *Gulliver's Travels.*

of a family of German diplomats. The gentleman was formally posted in Japan, and the house was full of Japanese objects: porcelain pieces, fans, and miniature gardens.

My grandfather, born in 1866, had lost his mother when he was just three years old during the last great cholera epidemic that struck Hungary. My great grandmother, some months before her death, had given birth to a second son, Uncle Charles, who was going to die almost a nonagenarian after my emigration. Uncle Charles was a journalist. He was proud of two things: being born on July 14, the day of the storming of the Bastille, and being born to a mother of the first ennobled Jewish family in Hungary. Mister von Keppich was an arms trader during the Austro-Turkish War of 1788–1791, and it was in recompense for his good and loyal service that he was attributed the title of *Baron*. Uncle Charles also recounted with great pleasure and arrogant satisfaction that one of his great aunts on the von Keppich side of the family was the mistress of one Prince Ypsilanti, a relative of the one who drove the victorious revolt of the Greeks against the Ottomans in 1825 . . . After the death of his wife, my great grandfather ended up remarrying, and from this second marriage came three more boys. The first, Uncle Edvárd, was going to become one of the glories of the family. A businessman, well-to-do, and generous, it was he that handled my mother's dowry and those of several of his other nieces. He died very young, but his widow and their children were able to leave Hungary, and that's the reason why I still have family in the United States and Brazil. In fact, one of the cousins from Rio married a Chinese woman from Hong Kong and currently teaches economics at a university somewhere in New Jersey. The two other boys, Armand and Marcel, were twins, familiar and affectionate figures of my childhood and teenage memories. As for Grandma, Irma Aczél, she came from a modest family of which I know almost nothing. Her mother, my great grandmother, knew me, but I've not retained any memory of her. The sisters of Grandma lived in a small provincial city, Szentes, and she visited them each year. (Before leaving, she ritually wrote a postcard announcing her safe and sound arrival.) Her two sisters were younger than her, but Grandma, who was going to die a few months before her hundredth birthday, would outlive them.

I have few memories from the summer of '43 other than those of visits to the house of my grandmother from Felcsút, who arrived in Budapest a little while after us. I remember also that we had spent some days in a boarding house along the side of the Danube, and I can vividly see the scene of an ill-fated waiter who let a tray of glasses fall and shatter into pieces. During the summer of '43, I began to read, or rather devour more books. I followed the normal course of reading for the Hungarian boys at the time: initially, the novels about the Indian chief Winnetou by the German writer Karl May, then a very large number of works by Jules Verne.[3] In the autumn, I had been enrolled into primary school. And of this, I have retained all but two memories. The first concerns a classmate, a certain Patkai Gyurka, with whom I was very close, but whom I have not seen in more than seventy years; the other, a catechism course, in which we studied the Holy Story. The young priest who presented it to us spoke of the Nile, which was supposed to have had its source in Egypt. I raised myself to the full height of my seven-and-a-half years to say to him: "No, Father, the Nile has its origin in Lake Victoria Nyanza in Uganda!" During these months of '43–44, I also remember a journey by tram, on which an old bearded officer was seated in front of us. I believe that the red stripe on his trousers indicated his rank of general. I was so excited that he addressed me in speech, and that he proposed we go to visit him. I didn't understand why Mama didn't respond favorably to this invitation. Another memory—ending with equally blighted hope—was of our visit to the Royal Castle. Admiral Horthy, the Regent, occupied a part of the palace, but another part was open to the public. To arrive at the castle, we took a cable car, which departed from very close to the Danube. I, who expected to find gold and silver, diamonds and rubies, had to note, with disappointment, that the furniture of the palace was not very different to that which was to be found in Grandma's house in Felcsút.

The year 1944 was the fatal year for the Jews of Hungary, and therefore also for my family. Hungary is a country of strong and solid antisemitic tradition. Under Franz Joseph, these sentiments were not able to become "concrete." But things were going to change with the collapse of the Austro-Hungarian Monarchy. In 1919, a communist republic had been proclaimed, which, during its three months of existence, exercised "the Red Terror." Among the directors of this Commune, there were many Jews. After the disappearance of this regime, antisemitism was unleashed into the country, and was also expressed by the law. The first anti-Jewish law was passed in Hungary during the Twenties: that of the *numerus clausus*, prescribing universities to admit no more than the percentage of Jews as students that conformed to the percentage of Jews in the Hungarian population, to wit, six percent. But, in those times, half of the lawyers and more than half of the medical doctors in Budapest were Jews. Likewise, there was a very strong Jewish presence in the banks, in industry and commerce, and equally in the

3. It was still during this summer of 1943 that, throughout the weeks which preceded my seventh birthday, I learnt to swim in the Saint Luke Pool, the pool of the good society of Budapest. Later, I saw Zoltán Kodály swimming there, his small blond goatee floating on the water. I saw Kodály again actually, nineteen years later, while at Oxford, where he told me how much the Hungarians detested their communist masters.

sciences and the arts. From the end of the Thirties, in part under pressure from Nazi Germany, the Hungarian Parliament continued to pass "Jewish laws" in order to restrain Jewish economic liberties. Since 1942, Jews were no longer called to military service, but to a "work service," where the conditions were unspeakable, and the atrocities, the executions, were frequent. This service was performed on the Russian front, where the members of these services died like the other soldiers. It was there that, in 1942, Uncle Arisztid, the husband of one of my mother's cousins, disappeared. Aunty Vera, who herself died in 2014 at ninety-eight years of age, was therefore a widow at twenty-six, and remained so for more than seventy years . . . The country, the Catholic episcopacy included, found it obvious that the Jews must suffer discriminatory measures. The bishops only protested against the application of these laws to Jews who had converted to the Catholic religion. However, during the years when the majority of the Jewish population of Europe had disappeared into camps and crematory ovens, the eight hundred thousand Jews of Hungary did not suffer any physical persecution (with exception to those in military "work service"). The Prime Minister, Miklós Kállay, a descendant of a family which traced its origins back to the 9th century, directed an anti-German politics. He couldn't institute peace, but tried to proceed toward it with the Western powers. Indeed, he protected the Jews in such an explicit manner that a delegation representing the Budapest Israelite community had gone to implore him not to provoke the Germans . . . But all of this came to an end on March 19, 1944. Hitler had invited the old Regent Horthy for discussions, and during these "discussions," the German army had occupied Hungary. On his return, Horthy was faced with a *fait accompli*, and had to appoint a pro-German government. From that moment, the fate of the Jewish population was sealed. The deportations began in April, and, in two months, some six hundred thousand people—all of the country's Jewish population, with exception to the community in Budapest—had been deported, and this, with the efficacious collaboration (often invigorated by enthusiasm) of the local authorities, despite numerous individual cases of resistance. Toward the end of June, Horthy had received messages sent from President Roosevelt, Pope Pius XII, and the King of Sweden (the eldest of the European sovereigns), advising him to place himself before his responsibilities. In March, Horthy had declared: "I leave to the government the task of resolving the Jewish problem." But he finally caught hold of himself and managed to prevent the deportation of the Jews from Budapest. It is by the grace of these measures that I am in the process of writing this autobiography.

Of course, I was too young to understand that which was going to come. First of all, we were prevented from studying at school (about which

I was greatly disappointed). From April onward, all Jews over six years of age were required to carry the yellow star in the streets. I remember that we had played hide and seek with non-Jewish children from the building who hadn't understood why I didn't want to hide *outside* of it, while my brother, who was not yet six, would blithely leave it . . . However, the people knew that the worst was yet to arrive. I remember a family from the provinces who managed to reach the capital. These people described the deportation to us, and also recounted murmurs about those deported being gassed. Obviously, we didn't believe it, because it was, and still is, incredible. Still, my mother, widowed, foresaw that our lives were in danger, so she decided to separate herself from me. I was entrusted to my aunt, Nita (Anna), and my uncle, Miklós. They were a couple without children of their own and loved me profoundly from a very young age. I called them Anya and Apa (Mother and Father) without any problem, and almost as if it were obvious once I was going to learn of the death of my mother. I went to them in the May of '44, while István, my brother, stayed with my mother and my grandmother. I think I saw my mother two or three times thereafter, for the Jews had the right to leave their homes during certain hours of the day. But in the month of June, István had contracted scarlet fever and was thus hospitalized. Mama visited him at the hospital, yet this coincided with a raid, and she was arrested at the exit.[4] She then spent some days in a transit camp in the north of Budapest. A Christian friend of the family made his way to this camp, but he had arrived too late. My mother was deported on the last train to Germany under the orders of Eichmann, and without the knowledge of Horthy. She was first in Auschwitz, then in a camp where women between eighteen and forty years of age labored to construct a large airport within proximity of Frankfurt. These laborers were "rented" by the SS to the German company responsible for the airport's construction. The names of these female laborers were recorded by the company on a list, and this is the only German document of which I am aware that mentions the name of my mother. She was subsequently transferred to Ravensbrück, and one letter that I received from the International Committee of the Red Cross in the Nineties said that this is the last place where there remains any sign of her presence. In fact, she had been sent from Ravensbrück to the little camp of Salzwedel to die. There, the commandant was a colonel, a good man who did what he could to lighten the fate of the deportees. But my mother was at the end of her strength, and she was therefore "hospitalized" in a shack that one would call

4. It was in exercising her vocation as a mother that she was arrested, deported, and imprisoned within a German camp, where she died, wrote Cardinal P. Erdő, Primate of Hungary (see Baranyai, "Nemzetközi konferenciával köszöntik a 80 éves Vető Miklóst").

the "Ambulance." Two days after the camp was liberated, on April 14, 1945, the breakfast sent to her was returned untouched . . .[5]

My mother was deported in the beginning of July. But I didn't know what had happened to her, and I confess not even remembering the absence of her visits. The summer brought a little improvement to the lives of Jews in Budapest, the only ones in Hungary who had not yet been sent to the extermination camps. Horthy had named a new prime minister, a general who was not subservient to the Germans. Of course, that didn't change the fact that the country continued to be occupied by her German "allies." The arrival of the Western Allies in Normandy in the month of June had certainly sent Horthy the message that the advancing Red Army, which had already occupied part of Hungary, was only able to increase in strength. Horthy would have wanted to make a separate peace deal with the Westerners, but that was no longer possible. So, he covertly sent a delegation to Moscow in order to ask Stalin for an armistice. And on October 15, he decided to take action, declaring via radio to have ceased fighting, while reproaching the Germans for the manner in which they had treated Hungary. But this armistice *coup d'état* was poorly prepared. On the afternoon of the very same day, the Germans disarmed those defending the palace, wounded the son of the Regent, and forced him abdicate in favor to Ferenc Szálasi, the leader of the Arrow Cross Party, and a fervent and faithful ally of the Nazis. Szálasi took the title of Leader of the Nation and declared outright war against the Soviets. Unfortunately, he had found collaborators, and not only among the ranks of his own party. This man, who had spent years in prison (for Horthy would not tolerate being undermined by the extreme right) was not exactly normal. He kept under his direction a large portion of the Hungarian army, with which he was, with the Germans, going to "defend" Budapest, and then the country's west. His government had to leave Hungarian soil on April 2, 1945. Having learnt of the death of Hitler, he subsequently buried the crown of Saint Stephen, the symbol of Hungary's history, and then held a Crown

5. In 1993, a Hungarian radio journalist interviewed me on the topic of my life events. Half an hour after the interview, a woman called him: "I was with the mother of this man from the beginning to the end. We were arrested at the same moment, and I was with her until the camp in Salzwedel." In fact, she had made contact with my family as soon as she returned from Germany. It was she who communicated to my aunt (who would emigrate to Israel) the death of my mother. But István wasn't really knowledgeable of all that. Subsequently, István and I went to Salzwedel. From the station, we were going toward the place where the barracks of the prisoners were situated, but had since disappeared. Someone was keeping his eyes on us through a window, and I had the impression that he must have understood why we were there. I returned to Salzwedel a second time, two years later. I talked with the people of the small town, but I think that their communist education had prevented them from understanding the past.

Council in an Austrian village. That took place on May 2 or 4, 1945. As the outcome of this council, he sent a telegram to Emperor Hirohito to assure him that even if Germany was going to surrender, Hungary was going to continue the war. And, in fact, the last war *communiqué* on May 9 had announced that combat has ceased everywhere, with exception of certain districts in Leipzig, where Hungarian units continued to resist . . .

The coming to power of the Arrow Cross Party sounded the death knell for the Jews of Budapest, who were going to be confined to a ghetto. Many men had been deported to Germany, and in Budapest itself those of the Arrow Cross Party imposed a reign of terror. They stood Jews on the edge of the Danube, shot at them, maimed and killed them, and their bodies disappeared into the water . . .[6] As for us, I remember that we were glued to radio set to listen to government announcements on October 15, but that the following day there was only silence: Szálasi was firmly seated in Buda Castle and the hunting of Jews was about to recommence. My adoptive parents thought it necessary to act, so, on October 17, they took me to a convent of nuns, which had in fact been serving as an orphanage. The convent was around one hundred meters from where the headquarters of the Arrow Cross Party was housed. And yet, this convent became a shelter to a growing number of Jewish children. My brother was to rejoin me on the following day, same with my cousin Gabor, now a reputable biologist living in the United States. The sisters were in the end even going to accommodate adults, mainly mothers. But I also remember an elderly "woman," dressed in black, who brutally beat the children. We ended up learning that this was a man . . . We were not overly happy in this establishment. The sisters were severely strict, we ate very poorly, and it was necessary to attend Mass at six o'clock each morning. This allowed me to learn the words of the Latin Mass by heart, yet it only instilled in me a very moderate sympathy for the Catholic faith. I have little detailed memory of the seven weeks there, but I remember well a visit from cousins who brought us books. I see even now my brother István stretched out on his bed, reading out loud. For he was going to learn to read as a birthday gift for Mama.

We stayed with the nuns until the beginning of December, when one morning my adoptive mother arrived to take us back to her house. The Red Army was nearing Budapest, and she thought that it would be better for us to be with her than at the orphanage. My adoptive father was deported, and the Jews who still lived in the building—I think of the women—were forced

6. My aunts Florence and Juliska were among the Jews arrested and taken to the Danube to be shot. But Aunty Juliska had understood what was going to happen. She thus said to her cousin: "Come, let's run." They were shot at, but the bullets missed them.

into the ghetto. The concierge, a simple woman, received my brother and I along with a small amount of money. We were at peace, tranquil, while elsewhere the Arrow Cross Party continued to take Jews to be shot at the edge of the Danube.[7] Simultaneously, the Russians ended up encircling the capital, but waiting. On Christmas Eve, we had a Christmas tree and some sweets. A cousin of my father, Aunty Izus, was employed in a candy factory, German-owned. And by this fact, she had right to German letters of protection. That is to say, the Nazi occupation authorities did defend some Jews from the Hungarian Arrow Cross Party![8]

After having received our gifts, we dined and settled into bed. But we were awoken by explosions. The Russian artillery was on all sides. Still, Stalin had decided to mostly spare Budapest from aerial bombardment, so there were maybe only some one hundred thousand dead, without counting the three hundred thousand odd soldiers of the Red Army. We rushed to take refuge in one cellar, and a few days later in an even deeper cellar. We stayed like this, underground, from December 24 until January 31. There were not, I think, but the women and both of us. And we no longer had any electricity. We were in deep darkness, faintly illuminated by candles. We had five minutes per day in front of a candle, allowing us to draw. The barrage of canon fire continued, but also some bombardment. Close to a hundred and fifty meters from our building, the Germans had positioned an ammunition depot. The Soviets, being well-aware, tried to bomb it, albeit without success. The bombs fell during the night, and although the noise of the explosions was deafening, the women could still be heard screaming in terror. I explained to them with the wisdom of my eight years that there was no reason to be afraid once a bomb had exploded, but, having no regard for my admonitions, these ladies continued to cry. One night, we heard an explosion that was particularly loud, later learning that the Soviets had

7. It was during these days that one of my future emigration comrades, Marika H., then only nine years old, was driven to the edge of the Danube to be shot. She was made to undress, keeping nothing but her underwear. The shots were fired, and she fell into the water, although without being touched by any bullets. She resurfaced and climbed onto the barrier, dripping with water. Alas, she found herself in the shadow of the very same man who had shot at her and the other Jews. She had thought that this was the end. But, seeing the little shivering girl, the man removed his own coat, placed it on her shoulders, and told her to run away . . .

8. The Budapest ghetto gathered some seventy thousand people who weren't able to be deported, including my aunts. The Arrow Cross Party had wanted to have it blown up at the moment the Red Army entered it. But it was a German officer who prevented the realization of this intention. Incidentally, this officer was going to die fifteen or so days later during the last battle around Buda Castle.

destroyed a different ammunition depot. This other depot was situated in a ten-story building. All that remained was an enormous crater.

The days passed, and the soldiers of the Red Army had already cleared the neighboring streets on January 16. At this stage, we had about enough to eat, but we didn't have any bread. There was, however, a bakery on the side of an intersection opposite our street, which, although no longer selling bread, did continue to freely cook bread that the people themselves prepared. Thus, one morning (that of January 18, I believe), my mother left with her dough. But she didn't return by the expected hour, and so women in the cellar told us to pray for her. She finally returned many hours later. Gunfire from Russian soldiers had prevented her from crossing the little street, that is, until the soldiers had moved further away. Only then could she reach us with the fresh bread, well-cooked.

On January 18, our district was liberated, and all the members of my family situated in Budapest, in the ghetto, returned to their apartments. Even though the bombings intermittently continued, more Arrow Cross militiamen continued to be killed. The Germans and their allies in the Arrow Cross Party had entrenched themselves in Buda on the other side of the Danube, and there managed to defend themselves for three weeks. One day, an elderly couple who lived in our building saw their children arrive. They had been separated from them and not since received any news of them. They began running to greet them, but a shell coming from the other side of the river struck these youths, killing them instantly. Also in our building was another old couple, Orthodox Jews, who could not obtain anything kosher. They therefore ceased eating entirely and died of hunger. Moreover, although the Russians had liberated the city and by this fact saved the lives of its Jewish residents, they also committed much evil. They plundered the apartments, and on top of everything else, raped the women—one of my aunts being a victim. I remember how a young woman, having been raped, spoke of such horror to my mother. I was supposed to be asleep, but in any case, I did not at the time really understand the discussion.[9] "The news" of the rapes spread rapidly, and, one day, at the sight of approaching Soviet soldiers, all the residents of the cellar fled to save themselves. Only my brother and I had remained when a Russian soldier arrived. I was terrified. As for my brother, he was too small for that. He approached the Russian and demanded to be shown his semi-automatic rifle. The Russians love children,

9. Stalin refused to intervene in this raping problem. "When a soldier has led the life of a dog, having constantly risked it," he said, "why refuse him a good moment with a woman?" Some months later, when the Russians besieged Berlin, the Jewish writer, Kapitza, an officer of the Red Army, wanted to put an end to these rapes. He was arrested and condemned to ten years in prison for "bourgeois moralism."

and this one was in fact happy to show István his weapon. I remember that his hand was horrendously dirty. Then he began to rummage through the beds and the mattresses, collecting what he found.

The Russians did not simply inflict harm. They knew that we did not have much to eat, so, from time to time, they arrived with food. I remember very well that they once brought us an enormous mound of tripe. This being said, the source of the meat was unusual: it came from the streets, which were filled with frozen horses. Even my aunt Juliska, who herself adored horses, went to carve large pieces out of them.

When the battles stopped, we were able to again find our apartment, albeit in an inhabitable condition. The windows had been shattered since Christmas Eve, and we obviously couldn't have them repaired. But we ended up finding a solution. The explosions had not blown out the windows of apartments facing the courtyard, so we rented a room in the home of an old lady (she must have been around sixty-five). We moved into her place on January 31, 1945. Some days later, my uncle Józsi (József—Hungarian given names are almost always diminutives), a doctor and the brother-in-law of my mother, had arrived to take István to his home. Aunty Jenny, Uncle József, their son János (later in Israel, Jona), and my maternal grandmother lived in a suburban house, where they hid, during the siege of Budapest, with false names and without carrying the yellow star. After the departure of my brother, I began to be bored. The school was still inoperative. And of this period, I only have memory of two striking events. The first took place in the month of March, when the social services of the capital once again began to function. A social assistant arrived with a large piece of white bread. I had not seen white bread for months. But my mother wasn't home, so I dared not taste it, as tempting as it was, until she arrived. The other event was the arrival of my cousin, János. This other János was the only son of aunt Irén (Ice), my father's sister. János was sixteen years my senior. He had been recruited in '44 into the "work service" of the army, and he did his service in Southern Serbia (not far from Niš, wherefrom, in the 4th century, the family of the emperor Constantine originated). He ended up breaking company with his unit, and succeeded in joining Tito's resistance, which prowled around German and Hungarian battalions. He did suffer from vertigo, but he was going to be cured of that. For he was proceeding on a narrow countryside path, with a handful of resistance fighters, when there had appeared Germans from whom they began to take fire. The path was cut by a small river, having only a single tree trunk as a bridge. To save his own life, he ran along this tree trunk without any sense of vertigo. Having returned to Budapest, János came to us. Considering the fact that my adoptive mother was not Jewish, we assumed that she had a greater chance of survival than the rest of the family . . . Some eight months later, my cousin, Marianne, daughter of Aunty Florence, my father's other sister, would similarly arrive at our house. She was deported at seventeen years of age to Mauthausen, but got away with some frostbite. Marianne did not know what had become of her parents, so her first question was: "Where's Mama?" We told her: "She is currently in Felcsút, at the house of her sister Irén." Marianne burst into tears: "You're lying to me! She's dead . . ." Her father, Uncle Bandi, a former croupier at Monte Carlo and a disreputable man, was not, even from a distance, a paragon of familial virtue. But when he had learnt of his daughter's return, he ran to a patisserie, bringing back a tray of eclairs. To him, his daughter was always a child to be stuffed with pastries. But that took place in November '45, and when she returned, we were still in the month of March.

Life began to organize itself amongst the ruins in Budapest. The war had begun to recede into the past. The Nazis and their Hungarian allies still occupied a large area to the west of the country, but that had no influence on the life of the capital. However, obtaining provisions was still very difficult, so my mother ended up deciding to leave Budapest to join her married sister living in the south of Hungary, in Mohàcs, the town where, in 1526, a crucial battle was lost, which was going to open the way to the Turkish occupation, and to the slow separation of the country from the portion of Europe that was progressing and enriching itself. My mother wanted to leave, but this was not so easy. We went to the station, where the rail services had once again begun to operate, albeit in an anarchical manner. Trains departed from time to time, but without any fixed schedule, and often without one even being able to know the final destination. Having arrived at the station, we boarded a train, but that train didn't leave. After waiting almost two days in a carriage, we learnt that another train was going to depart for the south. We were running to catch it, but it already began to leave. So, my mother threw our bags onto one of its carts, throwing me there next in the same fashion, and then finally climbing up herself. We had to change trains many times. I remember that one time, having landed on a coal train, I slept on the coal in an open car. It mustn't have been very warm, but that didn't prevent me from sleeping. It took some six days to cover around one hundred and sixty kilometers, and then we found ourselves in Baja, very close to Mohács, both being situated along the Danube. The family of Uncle Bandi owned a stationary shop in Baja. They had all been deported to Auschwitz and gassed. But we obviously didn't know that yet. We arrived in front of their house, which had since been occupied by the family of the shop intendent. These people were not very happy to see us, but they nevertheless accepted to have us lodge there for a day. Baja had not been bombed, and the town itself had suffered no damage. To be there was to live life as it formerly was. I was particularly overjoyed to find a bathroom in which the hot water faucet worked without a problem.

From Baja, we departed, traversing the Danube, for Mohács. Aunty Masi (Margaret) and her husband, Lajos, welcomed us with affection. During the weekends, we used to go to see their two children, both of whom did medical studies in Pécs, the birthplace of their mother, situated some sixty kilometers further west. Pécs is an ancient Roman city, filled with monuments, one of them being the only conserved Turkish mosque in Hungary. We had spent around five weeks in Mohács. Uncle Lajos, the husband of Aunty Masi, busied himself by running a wine and liquor store. But the store had belonged to Jewish landlords, and he was accused of having appropriated it illegally. He was all the time waiting to be arrested, yet still tried not to be caught by leaving every day to go fishing. They ended up finding him, however, and he was put in prison for one year. He was a very honest man, and I continue to think that he'd been unjustly condemned. As for his children, I've not retained but one memory, that of a brief visit. Ivan, as a medical student, had procured for himself a skeleton, which he brought back to the house in Mohács. He hid it in his closet, and then asked the maid to find him a shirt. When the girl opened the closet, the skeleton toppled onto her, and she ran away screaming. I must confess that I found this very amusing.

The five weeks in Mohács were going to refresh us. The weather was beautiful, and we ate very well. But Aunty Masi, in all of her kindness, was a bundle of nerves. She shouted at me, and her sister. My mother knew her, and after these scenes said to her, with little conviction, that we henceforth had no choice but to leave this house in which we were being vilified. Five minutes later, Aunty Masi would arrive with a guilty face and a tray of pastries to cajole me. I was shocked, and offended—but for all that, I did not refuse to taste the sweets.

We once again picked up our bags on May 7 or 8, and I remember that while waiting to change trains (which were functioning considerably better than they had been in March) we heard a loudspeaker announce the end of the war. Curiously, in that moment, that didn't matter to us, occupied as we were with finding a train that was departing for Budapest. We had arrived there safe and sound, but we didn't remain there for long. School had still not yet opened, so my mother decided to take me to Felcsút. Aunty Irén was already there, and István too. My maternal family didn't yet know that our mother was not going to return from deportation, and they entrusted István—in the beginning, I think, only provisionally—to my aunt Irén, who had already affectionately taken to him while my mother was still living.

Aunty Irén was a remarkable woman, upright and uncompromising. She wasn't in very good agreement with her sister-in-law, my (adoptive) mother, to whom she made rather unkind remarks. But this said, when, five years later, my mother needed to undergo a serious operation and we didn't have the money to pay for it, it was Aunty Irén who provided the doctor with all the money required. This was from her savings, which, after the confiscation of our goods by the Communists, were not renewable.

I was in Felcsút from the start of June to the end of August. Of our two houses, the small one, that one in which we lived with my parents, had become uninhabitable. The other one, that of my grandmother, was partially livable. It's there where Aunty Irén settled with István and I. The land reform at the beginning of 1945 had left us with a small portion of our land. Aunty Irén and her son János managed to have it cultivated. When the cereals were ripe, we had them harvested. And once the harvest was completed, all was confiscated . . . On the other hand, we were, provisionally, left the quartz mine. Incidentally, the pro-German authorities of 1944 didn't cut our ties to this enormous yellow basin. I also remember that during given hours of the day, when the Jews had the right to go shopping, my father regularly went to the bank to withdraw money. After the Liberation, we continued to tend to the property of the mine, that is until the end of '49. During the war years, we sent some two or three thousand wagons of sand per year. But, during the summer of 1945, the heavy industry had not yet again begun to operate, and we didn't exploit the sand but for local constructions. The intendant was the same cunning old peasant during the Thirties and Forties. I remember that the family used to say to my grandmother: "The old Szerencsés is stealing from you." And Grandma invariably responded: "May he continue to steal from us for *x* more years . . ." The old Szerencsés had been made a prisoner by the Italians in 1916, and I was excited to learn that his camp was situated on an island facing the coast of Somalia. It was the first time in my life that I had seen someone who had been to Africa, but he himself didn't seem to be overly interested in all this. Szerencsés was later going to come to Budapest each week to make a financial report. He ate with us—something inconceivable in the old days, when people such as himself hardly dared to enter into the house of my grandmother. Tragically, though, Szerencsés was going to die, aged seventy-eight, in a horrible accident: One day, while he was driving his horse-drawn carriage, it was suddenly overturned, killing him instantly.

During the three months of summer in 1945, I finished, at Felcsút, what was the equivalent of two school years. I was tutored by an old headmaster of the village, which permitted me to finish the academic year of '43–44, uninterrupted by the German occupation. But because I was even so still behind by one year, I also completed, during the coming summer, a third year of elementary schooling. It was the daughter of that headmaster, herself also a teacher, who had managed the accelerated learning. She also had me study catechism and spoke to me about sin and confession. I don't know how, but the question of very grave sins had been touched. I still see her face, full of worry and respect, explaining to me that there were certain sins that only the pope had the right to absolve. She hadn't specified which sins this concerned, and I suspect that she herself didn't know. At the end of the academic year, we found ourselves with the other young villagers at a concluding feast. The teacher posed questions that only I knew how to answer—a situation that was not pleasing to anyone else, and in the end, not even to me.

We led a modest enough life in the habitable part of the large house, still happy that a part of my grandparents' library had been preserved. But of this summer I've only kept a few scattered memories. Toward the end, I learnt that my adoptive father had returned from deportation. I fainted from joy.[10] I also remember that during my first catechism course, I had been quite frightened of the exhausting homework, which represented the obligation to learn by heart questions and responses. Another memory: In Hungary, one eats only little by way of aquatic animals, but I knew that we could have crawfish. So, I pestered my aunt until she ordered two youngsters from the village to hunt for these creatures. The two boys soon after arrived with a bucket full of crawfish. But, when Aunty Irén had learnt that she was going to have to cook these little beasts alive, she not only paid the boys, but also returned to them their crawfish . . . I was aggrieved.

Toward September 1, I left István and Aunty Irén in order to rejoin with my adoptive parents. My father, in the November of '44, after having had to march sixty kilometers, had been heaped together with other Jews in cattle wagons to be transported to Germany. The train had stopped at the border and there were Hungarian peasants at the station. The deportees were thirsty, so my father asked one of the peasants for some water. The peasant responded: "I would very much like to give it to you, but only if you give me your shirt. In any case, you'll no longer need it." He and his companions were deported to Bergen-Belsen, a concentration camp which was "credited" with the deaths of many hundreds of thousands . . . He owed his survival to a mistake: The Zionists had succeeded—I don't know how—to reserve a "special treatment" for deported Zionists. And my father, who for all his life hated Zionism and all that was of "Jewish consciousness," had been assigned to the barracks reserved for deported Zionists. He never

10. See p. 7, and n. 5.

wanted to talk of these five months. Still, he told me that one of the deportees, a Christian Jew, had him read the New Testament. But even though my father believed in God and sympathized with Christianity, he was not touched by the Gospel. By the end, despite his special treatment, the man who was a corpulent ninety kilos only amounted to a measly fifty. He would always repeat that he owed his life to a distribution of sugar by the Swedish Red Cross—authorized by Himmler when it was clear that the collapse of the Reich was imminent. My father told me that he had eaten the two hundred and fifty grams of sugar on the spot it was received, and that this is what had saved his life. He also kept the memory of an "SS guard" who was very humane with the prisoners. At the liberation, it was learnt that this was actually a British officer on an espionage mission. But, as for the conditions of the detention, the only thing of which he spoke was the superposition of many "layers" of cadavers in certain locations of the camp . . . On April 13, 1945, the American army was already close, so the SS had the survivors taken out, preparing to shoot them. In fact, there had been one hundred and forty-five dead during a parallel march. But the Americans arrived and hanged the SS on the spot. While waiting to be repatriated, the Jews were going to be lodged in German villages. My father spent around four months in the little village of Hillersleben, in close proximity to Magdeburg. Returning from this stay, he brought back a small crystal object to serve as a unique "souvenir." He thereafter repeated to me that he felt no hatred toward the Germans! That said, when I was to spend two months in Bonn in '65 to conduct research on Schelling, he would not cease writing to me of how happy he will be once I leave this accursed Germany . . . Still in the August of 1945, however, he didn't know if we had survived, and he was going to return to Budapest accompanied by a woman whom he'd known in Hillersleben. If I have understood well, he'd gone back with her to the building in which we lived, and, having learnt that my mother was alive, he promptly asked this lady to leave. We never again heard any talk of this.

The liveliness of Budapest had returned. One could once again eat one's fill. Two or three of the bridges over the Danube that the Germans had bombed—at least one of these bridges, the Margaret Bridge, having been blown up in broad daylight while many hundreds of people were crossing it—were reconstructed. And even the cultural life was put back on track. A grand exposition was opened in the Károlyi Palace, currently a museum, and I was above all passionate about its sculptures. It was in fact the beginning of a passion for the fine arts, a veritable love which still persists. My father was not musically cultivated, but he had a strong love of poetry, and above all impressionist painting. He had many friends who were painters, and he was proud to be elected as the legal adviser of a painters' association, the Ripple-Ronai society, so named after a great Hungarian painter (a friend of the Fauves), two or three early paintings by whom currently hang in the Musée d'Orsay. As a lawyer for artists, he often received his fees "in kind." I remember that we had once gone to see the great sculptor Medgyessy in his workshop, and it was I who had to choose a work! I chose a plaque, his self-portrait, which is on my desk as I write these lines. When, in 2011, I went to visit the Medgyessy Museum in Debrecen, I rather impressed the guards by recounting my memories concerning their hero . . . The return to school took place as normal, and I found myself with boys of my own age. (I was not going to have classmates of the feminine sex until attending university in 1954.) We had a master who considered himself to be a painter, and one day we actually had a class excursion to another school in order to admire a fresco that Mister Major had produced with another colleague. He was responsible for the drawing; the other, for the coloring. I don't have many memories of this school year. I didn't even have a true friend. We had a system according to which each week we had to elect three students to handle diverse tasks and represent the class in front of the teacher. The vote was secret, and to my amazement (and offence), my name didn't figure among those elected in the first week, nor among those of the two or three weeks that followed. Finally, my turn was going to come in November, but because of the cold and the absence of any heating system, the school was going to be closed for the entire winter. The courses stopped mid-week, and when we recommenced in the beginning of March, I finished the two days that remained of my term. So, to compensate for the fact of not having been elected first, I declared that I had been class "captain" from the month of November until that of March. The teacher laughed and even had the poor taste to ask me if I had actually attended school during the days of winter . . . We went to class from Monday to Saturday, from eight o'clock in the morning to one o'clock in the afternoon. At one o'clock, I returned to my house, after a ten-minute walk, in order to have lunch. At three o'clock, I left for the house of Aunty Florence, who lived at the intersection of our street, Tatra utca, and Saint-Stephen Boulevard, perhaps a hundred and fifty meters from where we lived. Aunty Florence had in her library the hundred volumes of the jubilee edition of the Hungarian Dumas, Mór Jókai, and I read, each afternoon, from three o'clock until seven (a period broken only by afternoon tea) one of Jókai's novels.

During the Christmas holidays, I went to Felcsút to visit István. I, who in the old days behaved a little badly toward my little brother, repented for the manner in which I had treated him. In fact, I missed him a lot, and I was happy to see him again. My older cousin, János Rudas, the son of Aunty Irén, accompanied me. We had taken the train, but from Bicske, we no longer had any other means of locomotion than our own legs. We merrily walked the five kilometers that separated us from Felcsút on a road covered by snow. The next time I was going to make this trip, although in the opposite direction, would be some sixty-five years later, with István, and we would encounter an enormous badger in the bushes at the edge of the road.

That year between '45 and '46 was the one in which I was prepared for my First Holy Communion. We had a marvelous young priest, Father Kalamaznik, as our catechist. Personally, I did not believe in anything. I considered myself an atheist, and I said as much to everyone. My adoptive mother went to see Father Kalamaznik to complain. The priest said to her: "Console yourself, Madam, for a boy this earnest will one day have the Faith!" So, I seriously prepared for the First Holy Communion. We went to Confession the day before, but I suddenly had the conviction that I had since continued to commit sins. I managed to catch Father Kalamaznik before the Mass to hear my confession again. He didn't seem particularly troubled by my transgressions . . . The only memory I have of my First Holy Communion was my joy in wearing a white bowtie, as was traditionally worn for this occasion by boys in Hungary. Another remarkable memory of this year is also religious in kind, or at least ecclesial. Cardinal Mindszenty, Primate of Hungary, made his entry into Saint Stephen's Basilica, where I had First Holy Communion. Wearing a miter and, I think, a *cappa magna*, he entered with a procession of clerics. I wanted to see him at a closer distance, so I attempted to push toward the front row, however a prelate put his hand on my shoulder and said: "When you are a canon, you can place yourself in the first row, but not before that . . ."

I passed the summer of '46 in Felcsút with István. Half of the house was still not habitable, but that didn't much bother us. We were happy playing, and with István, "to play" was a technical term. We began to invent stories, playing the roles of the characters ourselves. It was a time when we had to wait for all kinds of aid from America, and we dreamt about the inheritance that we were going to obtain after the death of our uncle Józsi, the orchestral conductor. We didn't know that he was already dead, nor did we know that he had been buried at his friends' expense . . . We "played" frequently about that which we were going to do when we grew up. I don't know why, but we predicted that István was going to marry, but that I would not, and that I was going to live with him. I was fairly impressed by this prediction, and István too. Later, in autumn, when István was staying alone with Aunty Irén, he would have her play the same game with him. Aunty Irén was the President of the Republic of Brazil, and István was going to ask for the hand of her daughter! I also tried to contribute to the education of my little brother. I decided that I was going to prepare a class for him, and that I would give him grades. In the beginning, I had wanted to award him with grades only at the end of the month, but I became more and more impatient. I thus decided to grade him as soon as the end of the week. But I couldn't even wait out this amount of time. So, I simply communicated his grades to him as soon as the first afternoon. The grades were rather mediocre. And they discouraged my little brother, who, naturally sour and recalcitrant, ended up refusing to continue these exercises altogether.

I had returned to Budapest for the start of school. In Hungary, secondary school began in the fifth year of studies. My father wanted to enroll me into the Piarist Fathers, the best scholarly establishment in the country, but I wasn't admitted. We thought at the time that this refusal could have been motivated by my Jewish family background. In any case, the refusal led to a choice which was going to determine my whole life. In 1946, Hungary was still free, at least as regards its internal affairs, and an announcement was made of the opening of a French section in a Budapest secondary school, Madach High School (on Barcsay Street), where my father also had done his studies (from 1904 to 1912). There was an entrance exam and I was ranked first (in front of three other Jewish boys, among whom one later became the director of the Frankfurt Opera, and another, a fairly well-known composer). The results were analyzed by psychologists among whom "the superior," one Professor Márai, would later become Vice Minister of Health. He continued to follow me from afar, and, ten years later, during an important political meeting, when the absurdities of the government's cultural politics were denounced, one of those who prepared the Revolution of 1956, an aide of Márai, took the floor to relate to the public that someone like me—I was also going to be a title-holder of the country's General History Contest—was seen to be refused admission to university.

I had been happy at the school. We first had six, then nine hours of French per week. In the last year, we had a teacher from Brittany, a communist. Mister Courtin had taught us French geography. I remember that he, in a rather distressed state, used to relate to us his culinary setbacks. In Hungary, we used to buy unsalted butter. (And, as it so happened, we didn't even buy that for long, because in '48, when the Communists took power, the butter rapidly disappeared from the shops.) Hence, having returned from the market with his block of butter, this poor man had to "spread" it onto the kitchen table in order to salt it copiously. The Hungarian professor, F. Závodszky, was a brilliant man, a polyglot. (In fact, he was going to end up as a teacher of French and Swedish in a specialist higher education institution.) He immediately noticed me, and I became his favorite student. I idolized him, and when, ten years later, I asked for confirmation, it was he who I was going to choose as a confirmation sponsor. My mathematics teacher, an old bearded man, was also a man of excellence. When he learnt that I read Shakespeare, obviously in translation, he expressed his conviction that I mustn't have understood much of it. I was wounded by these remarks, but I must confess that he was rather correct . . . As for the drawing teacher, quite the idiot, he detested and despised me. One day, when he told me off—"You must be stupid not to be able to do such simple things . . ."—I responded to him: "How come, then, I came first in the entry exam?" He retorted: "If the exam was to have been on drawing, you wouldn't have come first . . ." We had a lot of fun with him. One day, when he wanted to inscribe the names of three particularly excited students in the class' general register, his quill kept slipping: we had previously rubbed the pages with wax. I was, however, going to make peace with him four years later. On May 1, 1951, there was a festival for which the totalitarian communist regime had asked the people to march in honor of the party and the government. Every student and professor was going to march. In total, some five hundred people marched in the direction of Heroes' Square, where the country's leaders awaited them on an immense tribune. Only two people, the drawing teacher and I, marched in the opposite direction. It could have had serious consequences; I could have been expelled from the school, for example. In fact, I firmly believe that the success of the regime was in large part due to the cowardice of the people,[11] who dared not commit the least act of disobedience. And one would have been able to disobey. This same year, one of my classmates, who, although a poet and a chess champion, did not study but instead only showed his sovereign contempt for the school, had definitively enraged the principal of the establishment to the point that he was beside himself. This man had decided to expel the black sheep, but under communist regime, this kind of initiative could only come "from below." So, the principal called the four best students to his office and said to them: "We're going to have a meeting in your class, teachers and students together, and you are going to stand up to propose that Tamás be expelled." The meeting took place effectively, and my three unhappy classmates, like sheep, one after the other raised their voices to denounce Tamás and demand his expulsion. I was the last to speak. But I

11. This is reminiscent, keeping all in proportion, of Hannah Arendt's commentary on the rescue of the Jews of Denmark under the noses of the Germans. (See my "Cohérence et terreur. Principes métaphysiques de la philosophie politique de Hannah Arendt," in *De Whitehead à Marion*, 180–1.) When, in 1974, I was going to spend an evening at the home of Mrs. Arendt, she would tell me of how she had been detained in 1940 with German refugees in the camp of Gour, which was surrounded by a solid fence. She said to another prisoner that it would be worth trying to jump the fence. The other responded by saying that it would be too dangerous . . . But Hannah Arendt jumped over the wall and ended up being able to leave France for America. As for the prisoners of the camp, most among them ended up being deported to Germany.

said that although Tamás was indeed difficult, I wished for him to be given the opportunity to correct himself and take the right path. He was obviously still expelled, but I was not going to be reproached by anyone at all.[12]

The years '46–47 were relatively peaceable. Hungary had recovered its independence. Free elections had given the majority to bourgeois parties while the bloc on the left, under the influence of the Communists, had obtained some forty-five percent of the votes. But the Red Army was still there, and so was the Secret Police, led by the Communists. Rákosi, the head of the party, had already been, while very young, Commissar over the people of the Commune in 1919, which was defeated by the Roumanian Army. The communist leaders were refugees first in Vienna, then in Moscow. The Stalinist purges had decimated the Hungarian Communist Party. Its undisputed head, Béla Kun, was executed as a Trotskyist. Rákosi was found during this period in a prison in Szeged. Having organized illegal activities, he had been arrested and sentenced to life imprisonment. It was that which saved his life—all of his comrades were executed in Moscow while he rotted in a Hungarian prison. Finally, after sixteen years in prison, he was exchanged (with some other communist illegals) for the flags of the Revolution of 1848, vanquished by the Tzar's armies, having rushed to the aid of the young emperor, Franz Joseph. The flags were going to be displayed in the National Museum of Budapest. But, in Moscow, Rákosi found a bloodless party of Hungarian Communists, for whom he quickly became the leader.

Rákosi made his return to Hungary in an ammunition truck of the Red Army, but he had to bide his time. He began by trying to destabilize the government, of which he was himself a part. He and his comrades in charge of the Secret Police had fabricated a "conspiracy" trial with the intention of overturning the young Republic. The accused were mainly former generals, but certain characters of the Party of Small Land Owners, the most important of the parties on the right at the heart of the government, were also accused. The Secretary General of the party, Béla Kovács, was accused of having a part among conspirators, and when the Parliament refused to lift his indemnity, he was arrested by the Soviet military and deported to Russia. He was only able to return to Hungary after nine years in the Gulag, a little while before the Revolution of '56, of which he was going to become

12. Tamás Einzig, at seventeen years of age, wrote remarkable poems, and a theatre piece on Don Juan in magnificent verses (which would be published posthumously). At eighteen, he was married to another poet; she, aged fourteen. Having no means, they inhabited a cave at Gellért Hill. One day, Tamás said to Inez: "I love experiments. I'm going to take lots of sleeping pills: a quantity that will take me to the brink of death. Do not wake me; I'll regain consciousness myself." Inez obeyed. She didn't wake Tamás. But nor did Tamás ever regain consciousness himself. He was nineteen years old . . .

the minister. The arrest of Kovács had taken place still during this short period of democracy and economic restoration. The people were happy; the economy functioned. My father, as a lawyer, profited well. But all that would quickly change. 1948 was called "the year of the turn." The democracy was not formally abolished, but deputies, those who were not subservient to the Communists, began to be arrested, and many of them were going to take refuge in the West, the borders still being rather porous. Stalin had forced the Hungarian Government to refuse the Marshall Plan, which was going to permit Western Europe to regain its prosperity. As the atmosphere grew heavier, the people began trying to flee. My father had some clients, two young couples, who were preparing their escape in a rather extraordinary manner. They had a boat made that was supposed to represent Hungary in an international competition. The wives of the two who had the boat constructed had themselves been disguised as cooks, and the boat had to leave Lake Balaton in order to reach the Danube, with Istanbul as the final destination. On the eve of the departure, everyone was arrested, and my father was subsequently going to defend the two men, who were themselves going receive a prison sentence of four years all the same.

My father was close to an important journalist, Parragi, the deputy of a small party on the right, of which the head was Monsignor Balogh, a strange priest, who was also a member of the first government of Debrecen (1944), versed in affairs, and sold mainly paintings by the masters.[13] A Mass was celebrated in honor of Monsignor Balogh's twenty-five years in the priesthood, and at the end of the Mass, Parragi said to my father: "Tito and Yugoslavia are excluded from the Comintern, the international organization of the communist parties." Tito refused to obey Stalin, and Stalin thought that he could quickly finish with these rebels. Rákosi profited from the hunt for Tito's agents, for he had Rajk (the cruel and hated Minister of Interior, and his most important rival) arrested. Kádár, who was a friend of Rajk, had gone to see him in prison in order to explain that the international situation demanded that he confess his culpability. He was condemned to death and executed. Sometime later, Kádár was also arrested. He was going to be tortured, but he only received a life sentence . . .

During these school years, I learnt important things, but above all, a love for the fine arts. I remember having saved in order to purchase books on art. (The first of these books was a magnificent album, the *Trecento*, which I bought, I believe, in '48.) During all these years of secondary schooling,

13. A friend of my father was a deputy of the party of Monsignor Balogh. The party was moving in the direction of naming this friend Ambassador of Stockholm, and my father, Counselor of the Embassy, but with the suppression of the multiparty system, these intentions went unfulfilled.

the fine arts continued to captivate me. But, from the age of fourteen or fifteen, poetry took the place of painting. I myself began to write poems. Today, I find it odd that an adolescent of fifteen years does not write poems, even very poor poems . . . I had a passion for the great Hungarian poets, the classic ones as well as others of the 20th century. But in my eyes the most important poet was Baudelaire, whom I read and reread incessantly in the magnificent translation by three great Hungarian poets. Baudelaire has exercised an immense influence on my life. I even began to write a book on his poetry (I wrote about sixty pages of it). I adored the author of *The Flowers of Evil*, an adoration which almost cost me dearly. Baudelaire was counted by the regime as a bourgeois-decadent poet. But, at a high school literary circle meeting, I was going to give a lecture in which I said that the history of Western literature is divided into two epochs: one before Baudelaire; the other, after him. Evidently, that was a provocation. An alumnus of the high school, at that time already a university student, having returned to attend this meeting, declared that this kind of talking can only lead to anti-socialism. That would have been sufficient to warrant my expulsion from the high school, or worse . . . This university student, a certain F. F., was going to become quite a renowned member of the Budapest School, consisting of students of the philosopher Lukács. With four others, he would be expelled from Hungary in the early Seventies. But at this time, he was still a fervent partisan of the regime. Baudelaire was equally going to have a role in my spiritual progress.[14] This infatuation for poetry was incidentally also quite characteristic of the best of my classmates. I was overtaken by ecstasy in my reading of Keats' odes. Some of my classmates at the high school spoke of Heine and Lermontov, others still exalted the tragedies of Aeschylus and Sophocles. We read practically everything translated. I knew French rather well, but not well enough to be able to truly appreciate poets in that language. And the teaching of French—as that of all other Western languages—was in any case abolished in 1949, in favor of Russian. In Hungary, apart from a few former prisoners of war, no one knew Russian. Still, the professors of Western languages were forced to teach it. Our Russian professor was some five or six lessons further advanced than us . . . But I ended up persisting with this language for seven years. I translated some poems by Lermontov, although I knew not how to write nor how to speak Russian. Incidentally, after the Revolution and having arrived in the West, practically all the Hungarian students were going to forget the language. I myself lost my own understanding of Russian in about a fortnight. Apart from some lines of Pushkin and a dozen words applicable in everyday life,

14. See p. 36–37.

alas nothing remains of the language of our occupants. Later on, at Oxford, I was going to meet a North Korean refugee, a veritable linguistic genius. He spoke fourteen languages and taught Russian at an establishment in Pyongyang. Some weeks after his arrival in England, he was going to completely forget his Russian.

3

Adolescence—Szeged—Refugee Camps

Ours was the first state high school in Hungary. I must confess to not having kept outstanding memories of my teachers. With exception to Závodszky, these were not particularly eminent people. The class supervisor was a lady in her fifties, a teacher of mathematics. Another mathematics teacher, whom we already had in small classes, made allusion to a failed academic career. The teacher of history and geography was a kind but quite simple woman who knew perfectly well that I knew her subject better than she did herself. When she wrote statistical data on the blackboard concerning the countries of North Africa, she would correct them according to my remarks. Another geography professor, this one more competent, more knowledgeable, was responsible for organizing school geography competitions. I remember having rapidly listed the entire series of mountains that surrounded China, from the Himalayas to Manchuria . . . Obviously, I came first, and this competition was canceled shortly after. As for the general competition, I was candidate for history, and I should have brought back first prize, but this was 1954, and the Prime Minister was Imre Nagy, who was supposed to be closer to peasants. Hence, at the last moment, it was decided that the first prize should be awarded to a student from a provincial high school in the Great Hungarian Plain. It was, incidentally, a boy of Jewish origin, the son of a medical doctor, and having no rural appearance. He knew that he didn't merit his prize. Indeed, he even offered me an apology, and I was invited to stay with his family for a weekend.

Among my high school teachers, there was B., a very good specialist of Hungarian literature. Like many of his colleagues, he was intensely antisemitic, and, at his great displeasure, his best students were Jewish. One day, he said to Závodszky: “What a pity it is that one day, when the regime changes, all of these brilliant Jewish boys will need to be killed.” The only teacher of whom I’ve kept a touching memory is T., a German in his sixties, tired and sad. One day I met him at the edge of the Danube. He was walking with his mentally handicapped grandson, who had been abandoned by his parents (the son and the daughter-in-law of T.) when they fled to the West. Finally, I would like to mention László Pödör, the translator of Pascal’s *Pensées*. He was a brilliant teacher, a convinced communist who knew my “reactionary” opinions, yet he was not bothered by this and made fun of them quite gently. One morning, he didn’t come to deliver his class, nor did he return the following days. When we asked the other teachers what had become of Mister Pödör, they smiled lamentably without saying a word. We later learnt that Pödör had been arrested following the Rajk affair, and that he was going to spend many years in prison.

Regarding friends, I ended up having none who were very close. Fischer, subsequently Ferenczi, Laci (László), who died in 2015, was some months younger than me. He adored me for my literary culture. Having become a well-known historian of literature, he was going to tell me half a century after: “It was you who lent me *The Flowers of Evil*.” I also had much affection for F. Sz., who was a kind boy, although not very intelligent, having come from a simple background. I tried to help him as best I could. One day, knowing that a written test was imminent, I prepared for him a summary of the essentials of what we could be asked. The test began, but F. Sz. became distraught at the realization that he had forgotten to bring the summary from his house. I made another, which I succeeded in passing to him, and he began to use it. But the teacher who was supervising the exam noticed this paper in his hand and confiscated it from him. I was therefore forced to produce a third summary . . . His parents knew how much I was helping him, so his mother invited me for a meal of my choosing. It was an afternoon tea, but she served us *Turos csusza*: a plate of pasta with white cheese, fresh cream, and fried bacon. I took three large plates, followed by pastries! After the high school diploma, this boy was obviously not able to continue with university studies. He was admitted into health services in the army, and I met him only once thereafter. He spoke to me—as if it were something entirely normal—of an affair that he had with a girl in his formation. I was never going to see F. Sz. again. Forty-five years after our last meeting,

I returned to the front of the building in which his family lived, and I even found his name in the list of its residents, but I didn't have the courage to go to see him. In 2001, when I taught at Eötvös Loránd University in Budapest, I searched for his name in the telephone directory, and I phoned him. "Yes, it's me, Mrs. Sz.," responds the voice of a woman. I told her my name and I asked to speak with her husband. She said, "I know who you are. My husband has told me much about you," and then she burst into tears. Feri had just been taken by aggressive cancer of the liver, and this, sometime after the death of their only child in a skiing accident.

I earned my second prize in the general competition in 1954, and the laureates were welcomed on a two-week sojourn in a castle having formerly belonged to the counts of the Festetics family, the second aristocratic family of Hungary. Among these laureates, there was a young girl called Rózsa (Rose). She was nice. I even kissed her, and thereafter corresponded with her. I was a first-year university student, and she was still in the final year of secondary school. It was a little while after I began to live in faith, and she promised me to regularly attend Mass. But I had to tell her a short while later that it would be better if we ceased our correspondence.

This encounter took place during the summer of 1954, soon after I took the university entrance exam. According to the rigorous rules, the laureates of the general competition were to have automatic admission into the university. It is true that I was the laureate in history, but I had asked to study French literature. (The humanities were respected and sought-after! It was the Fifties!) The examiner, a French professor at the university, ended up telling me: "I will ask you nothing more, for you know everything." But, at this moment, my birth certificate fell onto the ground. A man resembling the Hunchback of Notre Dame, hitherto silent, leaned over to catch hold of it, saying: "Profession of father: landowner." He asked me with a voice as if coming from beyond the grave: "Is this your birth certificate?" "Yes, of course," I respond. After a long wait, I received word from the university announcing that I was refused admission. Obviously, I was devastated. I didn't know what I was going to do. But, my mother, who knew a law professor at the University of Szeged, who was also a party member, succeeded in having this gentleman intervene, and I was admitted into Szeged a few days after the term had begun.

The student who arrived at Szeged was a cultivated high school graduate, very metropolitan, but he was also something more: he was a Christian, a freshly converted Catholic, fervent, although not entirely sure, nor quite clear about what had happened to him. I was baptized, and I followed the obligatory catechism. But when, in 1949, this comportment had become facultative, while waiting to be frequently done away with, I, a convinced atheist, alone among the baptized Jews of my class, asked to follow the catechism. It was obviously due to an anti-communist tendency. Religion and churches were officially tolerated in Hungary. But, in actuality, alongside Cardinal Mindszenty and many other bishops, numerous priests as well as lay Christians were arrested and condemned to heavy prison sentences. The religious orders were dissolved in 1950. Most of the religious had to work in the world. Some were able to be redeployed in parishes. And generally speaking, to be Christian, to practice faith, had become dangerous. I was an atheist, but from the age of fourteen or fifteen, I began to slide toward a position that was more open, let us say agnostic. The simple fact that the Communists persecuted the Church and violently attacked religion gave me a kind of sympathy for it. At fifteen years, I read *Madame Bovary*, and the character of Homais, the pharmacist, instilled in me for good a contempt for these vulgar Voltaireans. Finally, my respect and unlimited admiration for Baudelaire, a Christian poet, rendered to me intellectually respectable all of that which formerly seemed to me to be so much ridiculous obscurantism. However, all of this only raises a negation: religion no longer appeared ridiculous to me. But I still had no feeling that called me to become a believer. That is, until one day in February 1954. It was a Wednesday afternoon (the third Wednesday of the month, I believe), and while crossing Saint-Stephen Boulevard, some two hundred meters from my home, I received the imperatival conviction of needing to attend Mass. Not knowing that Mass was celebrated during the week, I had to wait until Sunday. I went to Mass at a grand chapel, some three hundred meters from our apartment, and since that day, I've not ceased going to receive the Eucharist.

Of course, things weren't so easy. My family, without being explicitly opposed to this turn toward the faith, did not understand. Adults in the family spoke of my "religious delirium." As for my classmates, none shared this new dimension of my existence. And as for me, I understood nothing at the Mass. In fact, the liturgy bored me. And I simply didn't think about personal prayer. One day, I went to see the curate in charge of the chapel in order to pose this stupid question to him: "Father, how does one acquire faith?" He replied to me: "If I knew, I'd write a large book explaining it . . ." Still happy, I wasn't stopped by the response of this kind priest, and providence did what was necessary. A little while later, I read Pascal and fell upon a passage saying something like this: One couldn't know that God exists if one didn't have the Faith; one need only place oneself upon one's knees, and one will pray, and one will believe.[1] That made me understand I had to

1. See Pascal, *Pensées*, 418.

persevere, to continue to attend Mass at which I was unquestionably bored. And in this way, my faith would be stabilized, illuminated . . .

The founding experience, without any reason, without how or why, took place while in Budapest, and it was still there that this passage in Pascal permitted me perseverance. But it was in Szeged that my faith was going to be strengthened and magnified. First, nothing changed. I was attending Mass at the cathedral, but I knew no one among those who practiced faith. I had obtained—which was an exploit in these times of real socialism—a copy of the New Testament, and I put myself to reading it. I didn't know how one was to read the Scriptures, but I remember having been struck by the beatitudes. There, it was the first time that my faith, without content, without a why, received a thetic expression. I was profoundly taken, seized by this dialectic of strength and weakness, by this irruption of transcendence into the world. From that moment, the time of its primary conceptualization, faith has been the without-reason [*le sans raison*], the without-why [*le sans pourquoi*], the pure gratuity [*le gratuit pur*] . . . It was at that time, in the autumn of 1954, that, one afternoon, I put myself on my knees in Cathedral Square . . . only to quickly get up again. A short while later, during Mass at the cathedral, I experience a levitation: I had been elevated a few centimeters—perhaps ten or twenty (I'm not sure exactly)—above the ground. Perhaps one year later, when I began to go to Confession with the marvelous Father Vass, I made him privy to this levitation.[2] He said to me, with an indulgent smile: "Yes, from time to time, God gives children treats . . ." During my second year at Szeged, I recognized that it was time I be confirmed. And during the Confirmation, I found myself amongst children. Six years later, in France, when I had to furnish documents in preparation for marriage, I wrote to the parish in Budapest where I had been baptized to request my certificate of baptism. How astonished I was to notice an insertion: "He was confirmed in May, 1949." This complete "forgetfulness" bears witness to the almost nonexistent traces left by the religious instruction of my childhood.

But it was the meetings with other students that permitted the coming to fruition of my religious life. I took courses in German and French at the university in which I made the acquaintance of a student a little older than me. Feri Kiefer studied mathematics, but he also seemed to do and know everything else. He took courses in medicine and played chamber music, and he read in five or six languages. Later, he was going to become a world-renowned linguist, and until very recently President of the International Society of Linguistics. He was also going to become a member of five different European academies. And, on top of all that, he knew how to

2. See p. 40.

prepare rillettes and snail . . . Feri was the center of a small group of students, old classmates of his hometown of Baja, who met in his room twice per week. One of the weekly meetings was to listen to music; the other, to talk "philosophy." Alas, music was, and was going to remain, an unknown domain for me. (I have problems with my balance organs, and perhaps that is the origin of my radical insensitivity to music.) Once or twice, I felt pleasure during these evenings of music, notably while listening to Haydn's *Creation*, but things didn't progress past that. My wife, Odile, loves music. All my friends are lovers of the opera and concerts, and yet I am still alien to this world. However, if the music meetings didn't do much for me, it was going to be another story entirely with the philosophy meetings. Feri was a student and a disciple of a Hungarian philosopher, L. Gondos-Grünhut, an authentic mystic. From Jewish origin, Gondos was converted to Catholicism, which he practiced until his death. But what was essential for him was the religious experience of God, about which he spoke with an unforgettable fervor and concentration. Of course, he didn't only speak about it. He also wrote of it. After his studies in science at the Sorbonne, he completed studies in psychology and philosophy at Marburg. He published two beautiful books at the age of twenty-nine, works that the famous German Catholic philosopher, Przywara, was going to compare to the writings of the young Saint Augustine, and which Hans Urs von Balthasar cited still in his later writings. Gondos, who had envisaged a *Habilitation* at Fribourg, instead returned with his family to Hungary. His letter of rejection, which contains a single sentence by Heidegger, has not been lost. Having survived the compulsory "work service," he was, after the war, offered a university chair—provided that he join the Communist Party. In the face of his refusal, he was transferred to a primary school. During these dark years of Communism, Gondos united the youth and provided them with lectures in philosophy: commentaries upon the great Greek, Hindu, and biblical texts, which he interpreted as so many ways toward God. After the Revolution, he took refuge in Germany, and at the age of fifty-nine, he succumbed to cardiac arrest. I managed to publish a German anthology of his writings, entitled *Die Liebe und das Sein* [*Love and Being*],[3] which has recently also appeared in Hungarian. In a philosophical epoch dominated by the Heideggerian quest for Being, Gondos announced the maintenance of Being above Nothingness by Love, by God. I was never tempted to adopt Gondos' theological principles, but this spiritual metaphysics gave much to me. It is a thought that brings awareness to spirituality, to the divine, but which,

3. Gondos-Grünhut, *Die Liebe und das Sein*. The anthology has also appeared in Hungarian. In French, see my article "L'Être et l'amour. Introduction à la pensée de L. Gondos-Grünhut," in *De Whitehead à Marion*, 115–35.

in the capacity of theological doctrine, is only truly imaginable for certain individuals having experienced personal spiritual-mystical encounters.

Another encounter in Szeged was with János Aszalós, the closest friend I had. I found myself in a dentist's waiting room, reading a collection of medieval spiritual hymns, and János made a remark to me. This kind of reading was not something formally prohibited, but neither was it something really recommended. János had just completed his three years of military "work service," the Communists having instituted it as well, for it represented a kind of continuity with the Horthy regime. Obviously, those called didn't risk death—there was no war—but neither were they treated very well. János had first been a Cistercian novice. Following the dissolution of the order in 1950, he was able to enter into a diocesan seminary, which he subsequently had to leave. After three years of "work service," he had himself admitted into university to do mathematics, but he did not lose sight of the possibilities of an apostolate, and I represented one. We found each other again after our meeting at the dentist, and since that time—for over more than sixty years—we have lived in fervent friendship.[4] János had me read the great dogmatics of A. Schültz, a classic dogmatics, well structured, and to my eyes fascinating. I can still see the distressed face of the librarian at the university when she had to give me the work that had arrived from the shelves at my request . . . This scholastic treatise taught me to consider faith as explicable by knowledge. I had difficulties with subtle distinctions in the exposé on the doctrine of grace, but I devoured the rest with fascination, notably the teaching on the attributes of God, and the transcendentals (the good, the true, the one). However, more important than that of dogmatics was my discovery of the Spanish mystics. János introduced me to Father Vass, the spiritual director at the seminary in Szeged. Father Vass found that the persecution of the Church was in the end a good thing. If not, he said to me, we would again fall into a type of confinement in the "societies of the altar," appreciated by pious ladies of the good society. Now, he said, faith has instead become an affair of existential engagement. This profound priest was nourished by the authors of Carmelite mysticism, and he also nourished me with the texts of these writers, most notably those of Teresa of Avila and John of the Cross. For me, John of the Cross was the essential author. All while going each morning to Mass, I still believed myself to be subject to "doubt." But, John of the Cross explains to us that we must not search for manifest certitude or manifest consolation, but live in "the darkness of faith." After around fifteen days of reading John of the Cross, I

4. János died in August 2016. I was able to render him a farewell visit some six weeks before his death.

understood that my doubts concerned psychology, and consequently *myself*, while the Christian faith is an affair of "objective" truth, professed by the Catholic Church, the Church of Jesus Christ, infallible depository of the Faith. I arrived at this position sixty years ago, and it has not changed. May the Lord be praised!

At Szeged, I undertook studies in law. The Faculty of Law was a garbage dump. No one wanted to go there. In the past, it had been the breeding ground of lawyers, but who would want to become a lawyer in a country where the last surviving relics of private property were in the process of being done away with? We were a total of seventy in first year law. As for the law itself, it is learnt by heart. Hence, I was able to read almost throughout the entire semester, putting myself to study only a few weeks before the exams. One had, therefore, all one's time to read. We had excellent professors, including a famous old man, an academic and great specialist in international law, who ignominiously and uselessly enslaved himself to the regime that would have in any case been kind toward and even praised him. The majority of the professors began their careers while still in the Horthy regime, but a certain number among them were assisted by students just a little older than us. They were typically young workers or peasants, chosen for their fidelity to the regime. They were rather suspicious in my regard. However, one of them, who was already an assistant and had to do practical work in international law, had learnt that I read French. Rather embarrassed, he asked me whether I could help him with his work. The library of our institute possessed an excellent manual of international law, alas the book was in French. He asked me, therefore, if I could make summaries of some chapters for him. I complied, and he wanted to compensate me. One day, he called me into his office: "Miklós, it seems that you go to Mass?" I responded: "Indeed . . ." He looked at me with a concerned face and said: "Miklós," I advise you to "change your ideology" (*Weltanschauung*).[5] Around thirty years later, when Communism had collapsed, as a seasoned professor and former dean, he was going to be sent into retirement.

During the first years of our legal studies, we had not but general courses: Roman law, history of law, philosophy of law. The professor of Roman law was a famous lawyer in Budapest, one of the leaders of a small radical party, which was never formally dissolved, and which kept its premises, where Master Halasz continued to receive his clients. He lived in Budapest, but on one day, he would take a plane to Szeged, on another day, to Pécs, where he was also a professor. He smoked long luxurious cigarettes and delivered magnificent classes. I remember most notably one of his seminars:

5. "Miklós, You Should Change Your Ideology," 144–7.

servitudes in Roman law. When he learnt that I had become a believing Catholic, he was staggered . . . "Be Catholic, sure, if it is in order to obtain a good ecclesial benefit, but if not, why? What's more, these people are those who killed your parents . . ." Like him, my philosophy of law professor was also Jewish. He was a monument of opportunism. As a son of the richest fish trader in Szeged, he was, according to all appearances, a fervent communist. This was the epoch in which Tito and the Yugoslavian Communists were considered to be enemies of true socialism, lackeys of American imperialism. But, in September 1956, Khrushchev had gone to visit Tito, and the USSR and Yugoslavia were reconciled. Two days after that reconciliation, one saw large posters on the city walls: Professor Antalffy, great specialist on the Yugoslavia of the people, would deliver a lecture on the Yugoslavian path toward socialism . . . A little while after the squashing of the Revolution of 1956, yet still at a time when the people were hopeful for change, Antalffy became an "adviser" of the Kádár Government: He had understood well before the rest of the Hungarian people that the Kádár regime was going to last . . . Still before the Revolution, he had invited me to a café to take a glass with him. I began to complain: "What is it that I'm going to become after the end of my studies? I don't want to practice law, and, given my 'social origin,' I will never be recruited in academia." Antalffy responded to me: "Who knows what will happen between now and a year from now?" And yet the strength of the regime maintained the belief of its permanence, which it inculcated in the people. I would see Antalffy again, albeit for the last time, twenty-eight years later: As a professor at the University of Rennes, I returned to Hungary in order to deliver lectures, but I was also going to visit my former professors. He, radiant with joy to see me again, wanted me to taste a particularly delicious apricot juice. Then he placed in my hand two large volumes that together constituted a study on Machiavelli in French. "Here, take these," he said to me, "and if they are too heavy, you only have to ditch them before your return flight to Paris."

The only material which truly interested me was that of the history of law. But instead of studying laws and contracts of medieval Hungary, I threw myself head first into the study of Babylonian law. I fetched books in German and French from Budapest and drafted a short piece on the Code of Hammurabi, the first known collection of laws. That is why, incidentally, once I had arrived in Paris in '57, my first visit to the Louvre would commence with contemplation before the cut stone which carries the text of the Code! Obviously, I recognized that in order to study Babylonian law, it would be a requirement to begin an apprenticeship of the language in which it has been written. I had gone to see the old professor David in Budapest, a great specialist of this vanished civilization. He gave me quite a chill in explaining to me that cuneiform writing had been practiced for almost three millennia and that each sign had many variants according to the time. He himself had worked with cuneiform over some thirty years, but he could only read, without problems, those tablets coming from the epoch that he had studied. Seeing that I was persisting, he told me to first begin studying the six hundred "simple signs." Consequently, I tried to copy and learn these signs during my university courses. One of my classmates, with vulgar simplicity, said to me: "You don't even know English; why therefore learn Babylonian?" Alas, I didn't get very far with my apprenticeship of cuneiform. The only fruit of these studies was gathered three years later, in Paris. I was completing my History of Religions examination, and I chose as a topic for an oral presentation the religions of the ancient Middle East. I was interrogated by Dupont-Sommer himself, a famous specialist of the East, who had left the priesthood before the Great War. He was accustomed to hearing some scraps of history presented by poorly prepared students, but I began by reeling off explanations of the Anunnaki and the Igigi, who, as everyone knows, were the Babylonian demi-gods. At this moment, he stops me and asks: "Where did you learn that?" In the end, he prophesied to me: "Young man, you will go far . . ." My interest for the ancient East also drove me to read a work on the monotheistic pharaoh Akhenaten, and I put myself to translating, from the German, hymns to his Sun-God. Very recently, I stumbled upon the notebook that contains these translations, and I read with stupefaction my introduction, which almost centers on the question of the freedom of God, a theme which captivated me one quarter of a century later. At Szeged, I read many new texts, namely those mystical and religious, and I of course continued to study the great Hungarian and foreign writers. In addition to the classic authors of Hungarian poetry, Ady, Arany, and Vörösmarty, and the incomparable Baudelaire, I had been, since my youth, stimulated by the tragedies of Sophocles and Aeschylus. I would be enchanted when I read, some years later, a text of Barbey d'Aurevilly declaring: "I honor the Greek tragedians, Aeschylus and Sophocles, but not Euripides." I, the same; I found Euripides beneath them and above all too psychological.

I very much loved the Hymns of Callimachus, the Latin poets Catullus and Ovid. I tried to read Dante, but I stalled in the middle of the Purgatory. I wasn't going to finish reading *The Divine Comedy* until some fifty years later, in the mountain cabin where I'm writing these lines. As for novelists, outside of some great masters of prose such as Mikszáth, I read much of Balzac and Stendhal. But it was above all Russian literature that enthuzed me. I read (in translation) Lermontov and Pushkin. I devoured Tolstoy. But the *summum* was Dostoyevsky, and I found his *Brothers Karamazov* to be the greatest novel of all time. When I reread it some twenty years later while on the Soviet liner that brought us back from New York to Europe, I confess having been a little less enthused by it. I also read Thomas Mann, the entirety of his novels and novellas. I remember, while sitting on the balcony of our apartment in Budapest as a seventeen-year-old high school student, having "completed," in two days, the sixteen hundred pages of the biblical tetralogy, *Jacob and his brothers* . . .

However, philosophy and spirituality, as well as the change of language, were going to alter my relation to literature. Since Szeged, I've only read novels in the evening, and as regards poetry, I only reread the Hungarian poets (poetry, alas, didn't do much for me in French or English). In any case, I ceased writing poems from the moment of my arrival in Szeged. It is true, I made a start on an autobiographical novel, but after some sixty pages, written almost in a trance, and without leaving my room, not even to eat, I abandoned this story. And the text has since disappeared.

Material life in Szeged was rather poor, but in the end satisfying. In the beginning, I was lodged in a student house: we were in total twelve in one dormitory. Thereafter, I changed residence to a miniscule building situated in the garden of a family of German origin. The building was very close to a small pigsty, and my friend, Kiefer Feri, had long persisted in saying that I lived *with* the pigs. Regarding meals, I took them at the university restaurant: the food was vile, and insufficient. The person who collected the tickets passed between the soup and the *plat de résistance*. It was at this moment that some of those among us hurriedly got up and left, without giving the required ticket. I ended up deserting this restaurant to have my "meals" in a kind of dairy, wherein one was served yogurt, bread, and pastries. Put briefly, these were meals for young girls . . . I wasn't dying of hunger, but neither was I overly nourished. The idea of going to a proper restaurant never passed through my head.

Throughout my time in Szeged, I stayed in close contact with my family. I returned to Budapest in order to visit them at least every other month. The truth is that in Szeged, I felt very well, free—free from the (alas tiresome) affection of my adoptive parents. Once having returned to their home, they didn't want me to go to see any other family or friends: they didn't want me to move from the apartment. And their poverty was such that they refused to let me make phone calls. On the other hand, because I had a good scholarship, I proposed that they let me pay for my communications—a suggestion they weren't inclined to accept. The result: I had to go to public phonebooths to be able to call people . . . At the end of my first year of studies, I was called "under the flag." Each summer, the students had to do one month of service, and after obtaining their diplomas, six additional months in order to be named reserve officers. We had our camp not far from Balaton. We had uniforms, including patches. We were made to shave our heads (most of my comrades being devastated by this). And we also slept in tents. But we were supervised by stupid sub-officers who had considered bothering us to be the essence of their professional responsibility. They were accustomed to "normal" recruits, and we represented the country's future elite. Also, the fact that they knew we despised them didn't help things . . . Still, we learnt to handle arms and were made to shoot at targets. But as for me, they instantly saw that they were not dealing with someone very gifted. On one occasion, they had me shoot, and then said: "Go and see your results on the target." I ran to see; and, rushing back, I announced proudly: "I got nine out of ten." The sub-officers then burst into laughter. They had in fact made me shoot at targets used by the chap before me. The other students were also made to lance hand grenades; but not I. I think they had too much fear that I would blow myself up, and that I would blow the others up with me. But when we had nothing to do, with the ground around our tents being blanketed with leaves, they ordered us—me included—to *sweep* the forest.

But I also had more serious problems. The exercises were directed by officers, assisted by sub-officers. One day, the lieutenant under whose command I was shouted at me. And, turning toward the sub-officers, he intimated the order to henceforth make my life difficult. Returning his gaze to me, he announced: "You will have a difficult life. You will have to pray to your God for Him to help you." Then, after two moments of pause: "Do you have a God?" I remember standing up straight to tell him: "Yes, comrade lieutenant." From that moment on, no one bothered me, and when I appeared fatigued, the lieutenant carried even my rifle. I would learn a little later that he was a believer.

Still, little of this pleased me, so I decided to attempt to have myself exempted from service by simulating an illness. I went to the military doctor who listened to my vague complaints. He asked me: "Do you like playing chess?" I thus had a sudden illumination: This man is bored and seeks a partner to play with. So, I announced in a loud voice: "Yes, comrade doctor." "Come with me," he said. He led me to the camp latrines, in front of which there was a rock paving like the squares on a chess board. For some days, I had the exclusive task of washing these slabs . . . However, he did end up sending me to the Budapest military hospital, albeit under the surveillance of a disgusting sub-officer who was going to borrow money from me (which, of course, he would never return). In Budapest, I was examined by another military doctor, who wrote on a leaf of paper: "Slightly nervous." Thereafter, accompanied by an additional soldier, a normal recruit, the sub-officer led me to the home of my parents. He should have immediately returned us to the camp, but, taking advantage of difficulties with the train times, he decided to go out on the town while the two soldiers under his orders were going to be confined to an apartment. I don't remember much about this farm boy who spent the day in our home—only that he asked my father if we husbanded pigs . . . on the second level of a town building . . . We didn't have the right to leave the apartment, but I couldn't resist the temptation to show off. So, I put on my uniform and telephoned a friend, asking her to come and see me. Agnes arrived in five minutes and collapsed with laughter upon seeing my get-up. The following day, with the sub-officer, we caught the train for the camp.

However, the story is not finished. I decided to profit from my visit to the hospital, and when the commanding officer of the camp asked me what the doctors had found, I had a sudden intuition. In Hungary, the medical prescriptions had always been written in Latin, and this is, I believe even now, continued custom. So, conjecturing that the lieutenant was rather limited in classical culture, I told him: "I have *Pragmatica Sanctio*."[6] The officer asks me: "What does that sickness entail?" "The inaptitude for all physical exercise," I respond. And, indeed, I didn't do anything more until the end of that month of military service . . . It's also true that among the hundred students of this "training," ninety-seven were named sub-officers. Me, well, I was one of the three who hadn't been promoted. Further, in the following summer, that of 1956, I wasn't even going to be called. I believe that they had recognized that the Hungarian People's Army, already in a way bad enough, shouldn't take the risk.

When the teaching period of '56 began, I made a start on my third year of university studies at Szeged. The year '56 was going to signify the change of my life, occasioned by the political turn of the country. With Stalin having died in the March of 1953, things had begun to move. In the month of June, there was a revolt in West Berlin, crushed by the Red Army, while in Hungary, the Communist Party, with assistance by and at the suggestion of Moscow, decided to reform the regime. Rákosi had to relinquish presidency of the government, which had been offered to Imre Nagy. Nagy himself was a "Moscovian" communist, come back to Hungary with the Red Army. As a member of the First Provisional Government (December '44), in the capacity of Minister of Agriculture, he had supervised the Agrarian Reform. Subsequently, he distanced himself from Rákosi and no longer had any important function. But, above all, he began to take measure of the disaster of the tyrannical, lawless regime of the Party, which also destroyed

6. The *Pragmatica Sanctio* was the law of 1723 which had admitted the possibility of royal succession by the feminine side of the Habsburg House. The story is told in the autobiography of my late comrade, Czigány Lóránt (*Ahol állok, ahol megyek*, 358).

the country's economy. Nagy gave an inauguration speech announcing the closure of the internment camps and the break with the dictatorial methods of the regime, while declaring to understand the difficulties and the bitterness of the peasants. My father listened to this speech at the home of a friend—we didn't even have a radio—and he returned to us announcing to anyone who would listen: "Communism is finished in Hungary." Unfortunately, that wasn't true. Certainly, many things were going to improve. The terror was going to diminish; the fear, reside. But Rákosi remained First Secretary of the party, and eight days after Nagy's speech, he delivered a speech of his own to announce the limits of the change. Thereafter, he exercised an undermining politics, and in the March of '55, Nagy would be replaced as government head by a young economist subservient to Rákosi, A. Hegedüs. He would remain Prime Minister until the Revolution of '56, which was going to bring Nagy back to "power," and it was going to be under his signature that the call would be made to the USSR to intervene in order to save socialism. It's also true that after the defeat of the Revolution, he would distance himself from the Party, and that in 1968, he would sign a document condemning the entry of the armies of the Warsaw Pact (USSR and its satellites) in order to finish with the Prague Spring. As for our government during '55–56, that would be a restoration of the Rákosi system without his worst excesses. But, in '56, the international situation was going to be altered. Khrushchev would denounce the crimes of Stalinism and promise changes. These changes would signify the end of the terror in the USSR, but in satellite countries, that was going to take longer, notably in Hungary and Poland. From '54 to '56, one was still conscious of living in a dictatorship, but the economy would show a slight improvement, and even if the arrests for political motivations didn't completely cease, one would have the impression of being able to breathe a little more freely. Of course, the Political Police, in Hungarian the AVO, continued to keep watch. And one day, Feri asked us to stop visiting his home. For the police had observed the presence of a certain number of youths in the building, and, in response, even posted a chap in the concierge's lodge. The paranoid police couldn't imagine that we wanted to come together for objectives other than that of conspiring against the regime. In fact, they weren't completely wrong: To speak of the Gospel and of Hindu spirituality was effectively something quite dangerous and powerfully injurious for Communism. Incidentally, the police surveillance wasn't going to last for very long, and so we ended up eventually recommencing our soirées. But in the June of '56, Feri left us. He had received his diploma with the highest honors. Alas, nothing is perfect in this world: During the final part of his examination, he was posed a question on his conception of the world, and, in response, he declared himself not to be a materialist. As a consequence, he was going to find himself in the college of a small town on the Great Hungarian Plain. At his departure, there were already around fifteen of us, and from among us it was me who succeeded him. I remember having been happy and having felt up to it. What worried me, however, was that I had seen that our history of philosophy course was inevitably going to lead us to Kant and Hegel; and at that time, I didn't understand anything about these immense thinkers who were later going to become the subject of many of my books!

However, our meetings were going to be interrupted for reasons much more menacing than my ignorance of post-Kantian speculation. The country was becoming aggravated by the regime, and as with every slackening of a dictatorship, the opponents of or quite simply anyone unhappy with this one rushed to the breaches that had been opened. In Budapest, a monstrous protest was held to celebrate the public burial of Rajk, executed seven years earlier. The former Minister of Interior had almost certainly as much blood on his hands as those who had him condemned to death, but the Hungarian people recognized in him a victim of the regime. And yet, even in that moment, one dared not put communism in question: the struggle was that of communist reformers against the Stalinists of Rákosi. In the capital, significant meetings took place, in which official or semi-official writers began to vent all that had accumulated during the years of the dictatorship. However, the first important non-communist association was going to be founded in the provinces, more precisely, in our university town of Szeged. I've always said that the Revolution wouldn't have exploded if I hadn't found myself in Budapest, at the home of my parents, during October 14 and 15. Two students, my friend János Aszalós and one of his comrades, suddenly had the idea to revive the MEFESZ, the former union of Hungarian students. They had come to ask for my advice, yet I was in Budapest. If I had stayed in Szeged, I would have told them: "You are crazy—that won't work." I was not a defeatist, but a realist. Thirty-three years later, I reacted the same way at the sight of the anti-Soviet signs in Vilnius, but at that time I would be wrong . . . But my friends had by themselves decided to go ahead. Thus, on October 16, in a large amphitheater of the rectorate, there was going to be a meeting held, the first in the country, convoked without any prior authorization, for the purpose of announcing the reestablishment of the MEFESZ. I, among many others, delivered a speech, and having now reread it in the recently published minutes, I confess to not exactly being able to understand what I had wanted to say.[7] What is essential, however, is that we

7. The monument that would be erected behind the university in 2007 to honor the revolutionary events would carry the effigy of each one of us. Regarding the general assembly four days later, see the photo on p. 71.

had asked for many things, and, above all, that we had decided to exist, to begin something new . . .

Meetings followed one after another. But I didn't have a role in the first plan. In fact, I had said to myself that it would be better not to overexpose myself: I was known as so unfavorable to the regime that my participation in the MEFESZ, or at least at the head of it, appeared quite undesirable to me. And yet I was all the same elected as one of the three members of my amphitheater's MEFESZ committee—third year of law. On the morning of October 23, I delivered a speech to put my comrades on guard against yielding to provocations and marching through the streets of Szeged. However, on the afternoon of the very same day, I myself was going to march with a great number of young men and women, all crying slogans. Then, suddenly, a rather muscular fellow approached me, seized me by the arms, and gave me such a kick that I was sent to the ground, at which point he said to me: "That'll teach you to participate in demonstrations against the Party!" I got up again, and, in all simplicity, I must confess that I fled, without any effort of ideological discussion . . . On this same afternoon during which we had tried to protest in Szeged, in Budapest, an immense mob had invaded Parliament Square. The Secret Police were shooting at the crowd, and there was a very great number of deaths. This was the Revolution. And at the request of the government and the Communist Party, which had been thrown into panic, the Red Army entered the country. In fact, a great number of units were already there. But we didn't know anything about that. The following day, the classes were suspended. There was a strike, more or less general, yet as regards reasons, we were in the dark. The telephone no longer functioned, so we were left to listen, stupidly, to the State Radio, airing talk of small isolated groups of counter-revolutionaries. That which also made us ponder was the incessant succession of government declarations calling for the insurgents to surrender in exchange for amnesty. It continued for forty-eight hours, many times per day.

After two strange days in which I was somewhat suspended by a radio set reeling off lies more and more absurd, I ended up again leaving my room. I only remember disconnected events. A meeting in a university amphitheater to hear a delegation having returned from Budapest made us understand that things were moving, that the fighting had ceased, that Imre Nagy continued to preside over the government, that Cardinal Mindszenty had been liberated from his surveilled residence where he had just been transferred from prison. (The other archbishop in prison, Monsignor Grosz, had already been freed during the summer, but the cardinal, who had refused to ask for amnesty, remained imprisoned almost until the start of the Revolution.) Perhaps the day after this delegation had returned, I found myself in the great room of the rectorate. Professors and students were in discussion when, with some concern, we saw that a crowd of people crying political slogans was approaching the building. We had understood that they were demanding that we remove the Red Star which decorated the façade of the office of the rectorate. The rector had just asked the fire department to proceed with this operation, but the crowd wasn't aware of this and was becoming increasingly menacing![8] So, having been lifted up by some comrades, I was hoisted through the window in order to announce to the people below: "Be calm. Wait. The fire department is coming." Once the mission had been accomplished, and I again found myself standing on the floor of the room, I must have had a very proud face, for the rector turned toward me to say: "You're a brave boy."[9]

The following day, I think, there was a protest in the central square of Szeged, during which the AVO shot at the people. I saw a young worker stretched out and motionless. His mother, thrown into a panic, had rushed toward him, still in hope, for kinds of reflexes were making the corpse move. Then a medical professor arrived, putting himself on his knees beside the corpse and placing his ear upon the chest. The mother was waiting, and an infinite time seemed to have passed before the doctor straightened up himself and turned toward her with an expression of desolation . . .

November 1 had been the turning point of the Revolution. Imre Nagy had declared the neutrality of Hungary, and the following day, he formed a coalition government with the participation of all political parties, emerging from illegality. We thought that Communism had ceased to exist, and that the country would again find its independence. In truth, the USSR had already decided to intervene for a second time. And this time it was for

8. The rector, D. Baróti, was a professor of French, and after the crushing of the Revolution, he was arrested, accused of espionage in favor of France. During the legal proceedings, the prosecutor said to him: "You invited the ambassador of France to visit your institution, and after the visit, you took him to the famous fish restaurant on the edge of the Tisza. During the meal, you and he left the room. Of what did you talk? Obviously, it was at that moment that you transmitted information to him." Despite the gravity of the situation, Baróti burst into laughter. He then explained that the ambassador had asked him where the toilets were to be found. But because the restaurant was still an extremely primitive establishment, he (Baróti), with some awkwardness, was forced to say to the diplomat: "Mister Ambassador, this is an old tradition in Szeged: those who come to the edge of the Tisza for the first time must pee into its waters." Unfortunately, the tribunal didn't want to believe him, and he copped one year in prison.

9. In November 2016, the University of Szeged awarded me the title of *Doctor Honoris Causa*. I was the eldest of the four being celebrated, and I was asked to deliver a speech. I concluded it by saying: "The window to which I turn my back while talking is the one through which I was hoisted to harangue the revolutionary crowd exactly sixty years ago."

good. To be sure, the Soviets had hesitated over many days; the members of the political office were not in agreement among themselves. But most of the foreign communist parties pushed the Soviets to intervene—notably the Chinese, and among the Westerners, Togliatti, who was in fact considered to be a moderate, an "open" man, unlike Thorez and Duclos, the heads of the French Communist Party. Togliatti was, however, certainly a cultivated man. But as for his moderation, that was only the dream of a people who wanted to believe in the development of the Eastern countries toward an authentic democracy, and who were firmly opposed to those whom they looked up with distrust, such as "anti-communist primaries." Unfortunately, the only veritable anti-communists are and were the primary.

At Szeged, I experienced the events of these early days of November in a kind of euphoria. Finally, we have won, Communism is finished, our country is free and independent. But for that, we needed to wait a further thirty-four years . . . On November 3, toward the end of the afternoon, I learnt—I know not how nor from whom—that according to military information coming from the southern border, close to Szeged, Russian troops had begun to enter Hungary. The morning after, Budapest Radio announces the Soviet attack, the protestation of Imre Nagy, and a war bulletin, according to which Hungarian fighter planes had engaged in action against the Soviets. The repercussions are well known. János Kádár and some of his friends founded a "worker-peasant" government in order to defend socialism, and they declared that only the entry of the Soviet troops could save the country. The day before, the Minister of Defense, General Maléter, went to the Soviet Military Command near Budapest in order to settle details for the evacuation of Hungary. At the termination of these discussions, he was arrested. And being one of those accused in the Nagy trial, he would be sentenced to death and executed. Nagy himself, with many of his ministers, took refuge at the Yugoslavian Embassy. Cardinal Mindszenty obtained asylum at the United States Embassy, where he was going to remain until 1971.[10] As for Nagy and his ministers, the Kádár Government negotiated with the Yugoslavians, offering safe passage, which permitted them to leave the embassy. Upon their exit from the embassy, they were taken as prisoners by the Soviets and deported to Romania. They were then going to be brought back to Hungary where, with exception to G. Lukács, the famous Marxist philosopher, they would be put on trial. In

10. Fifteen years later, I would have a student at Yale who was the son of one of these American ambassadors in Budapest during the Sixties. He would inform me that the cardinal had learnt English at seventy years of age just so that he could preach at Mass which he would celebrate each Sunday for the Catholics of the embassy. Unfortunately, due to his accent, his audience would still not understand much of his homilies.

the end, Nagy and three of his ministers would be sentenced to death and executed in the June of 1958.[11]

In Szeged, on the morning of November 4, the commandant of the revolutionary militia, Lieutenant Lazur, had called the people in order to distribute arms among them. He declared: "Those who do not want these arms can go back to their homes; it is not something of which to be ashamed."[12] I myself was scared, but what I feared even more was to be taken for a coward. So, I accepted the hand grenades and bombs that were offered to me. I returned home, and the widow who was lodging me asked: "What is it that you have in your towel?" "Look, these are bombs and hand grenades." "Lord Jesus . . . What are you going to do with these explosives?" "I'll put them under my bed." She was terrorized because she didn't know that a grenade which hadn't had its pin pulled out could not explode. I had all of this under my bed for several days, but I ended up giving it to people who I judged more apt to use it than I was myself. I am ignorant of what became of these bombs and grenades, but I don't think that they were ever used.

The students' revolutionary organization continued to operate, and we began to produce tracts.[13] Among these tracts, there was an *Open Letter to János Kádár*, which caused considerable ripples.[14] Some twenty-eight years later, having returned from France for a teaching "mission," I am on my way to the university and the taxi driver who was driving me begins to speak to me of the good old days of '56 and remind me of this famous *Open Letter*. I was careful to keep myself from informing him that he was in the process of transporting the author of this letter. Its addressee was still the boss of the country, even if the regime was growing weaker each day.

The salient event of these dead weeks of November in '56 was the appearance of *The Book*. This was a tome of four hundred pages, the second volume of a typed work, containing a list of the agents of the Secret Police in the provinces, the first one being devoted to those of Budapest. I was

11. In fact, one of the four, the young G. Losonczi, had died a little sooner due to having suffered terrible treatment.

12. Lazur was arrested, and after many sham executions, he was sentenced to ten years in prison. During the almost general amnesty of 1963, he was to be liberated. But he refused to accept his liberation. At the end of the day, he stayed, alone in the prison. They ended up pushing him onto the street and slammed the door behind him.

13. We had copied the tracts with the help of a method called "*stencil*." The device resembled a flatiron. One day while operating it, I received a phone call from a contact among the police: "The police will immanently descend upon you." When the police arrived, they found nothing but two students engaged in the activity of ironing their shirts. Concerning this event, see the enjoyable article written by one of my former students (Henry, "Veto Recalls Revolution," 2–3). It is reprinted in this book on p. 127–8.

14. See p. 113.

assigned the task of making a systematic summary of the personal data of these "agents" working in the domain of the churches, and the comments of their case officers. It was deplorable, first and foremost for foolishness: Each "agent" had been presented under a false name, but the rest of the information was exact. For example, X. Y., episcopal vicar, *unmarried* . . . Essentially—let us say, in ninety-five percent of the cases—it concerned people (ecclesiastics, but also those among the lay) who were subjected to blackmail, pressured to appear as though cooperating. And the case officers constantly spoke of useless information, limited to generalities. Once, one officer revealed his difficulties to his superiors. A priest, who until then was delivering intelligence, had expressed his desire to cease the collaboration: his conscience prohibited him from continuing. The officer's proposition: to "transfer" this Catholic priest onto the forefront of intelligence concerning Protestants . . . I was confined to my room for twenty-four hours, and I was only able to leave it once the work had been completed. It was not but recently that I had learnt that my summaries were to be used after all. They had been relayed to the provincial of the Cistercians, who, before his arrest, was able to put a certain number of his brothers and friends on guard. On the other hand, for the members of our "network," *The Book* had catastrophic consequences. One of them had turned traitor or had been betrayed by someone else. All the members of the network were going to be arrested and condemned to carry out heavy prison sentences (with exception to myself and one other, who succeeded in finding refuge in the West). At the end of these four mournful weeks, I ended up understanding that in Szeged, there was nothing more to be done. On December 1, therefore, I caught the train for Budapest.

The Kádár Government continued to slither forward, appearing to negotiate with the organizations born of the Revolution, which were still hoping to reach a compromise. Slowly, these organizations ceased to operate, and a great number of their leaders ended up being imprisoned. The National Union of Writers and the MEFESZ were those which had endured the longest. At the start of January 1957, we had a large national reunion of the MEFESZ, but the room began to be overrun by men of thirty to forty years of age, obviously emanating from the AVO. We voted, but being disheartened by the participation of all those present, we, the true members of the MEFESZ, ended up leaving the place.

In fact, I had been tempted to leave the country as early as late fall. A very great number of people had sought refuge in the West: people compromised during the revolutionary events, but also and above all many young people (and some less young) desirous to abandon a country in which the future seemed to be closed. I myself was also tempted to leave, even though

I had been momentarily restrained out of the consideration I had for my adoptive parents, who had grown old and had no other children. Still, we ended up deciding, my brother István and I, to take the train for the Austrian border, where we were going to work things out. At the last moment, however, István declared: "I'm not leaving. I can't leave Aunt Irén—she raised me." So, I also abandoned the idea of a departure, so as not to be eaten away by remorse. At the end of January, the classes recommenced at Szeged, and I had decided to continue my studies. But upon my arrival at the station, I found a classmate waiting for me: "You must get out of here as fast as possible—they are preparing to arrest you." I made an appearance at the university to prepare my escape, and on January 31, I actually left.[15]

This escape had been realized with the aid of Feri. After his refusal to claim a materialist *Weltanschauung*, he was named a teacher in the junior high school of the small town of Soltvadkert. His family still lived in Baja, some twenty kilometers from the Yugoslavian border. Nine tenths of Hungarian refugees fled over the Austrian border, but that was no longer traversable. The communist authorities had made the decision to stop the hemorrhage. Hence, they sent very important police and military forces to surveil the western border of the country. On the other hand, the southern border was not yet well-guarded. And Yugoslavia had showed its sympathy toward the Hungarian Revolution, for it signified an emancipation from the Soviet model. However, Tito had ended up understanding that it wasn't actually a reform of communism but the establishment of a multiparty democratic regime that he didn't want. He thus joined the heads of the various communist parties who were pushing the Soviets toward a second intervention, that which effectively took place on November 4. And immediately

15. Among my friends, János Aszalós would have two periods of several years in prison. The first followed the trial in which I myself would have been sentenced had I not managed to escape. The second was due to the great anti-Church offensive of the Kádár Government in '61. The reason for the arrest was the organization of a Christian-inspired exchange group, in which my brother István and our chemist friend Medgyessy participated. He was asked to confess that he had prepared the regime that the Americans would have installed in Hungary during an eventual war: György Medgyessy, at twenty-five years of age, would have received the Portfolio of the Interior; my brother István at twenty-three would have been awarded that of Defense . . . Prison under the Kádár regime was no longer the place of terror that it was under Rákosi. There was even regular formation for prisoners who hadn't finished their elementary studies, and the prison guards themselves were able to profit from this teaching, which was presented by those being detained with teaching diplomas. János was a teacher of mathematics, and when he wanted to confess, he would ask to see one of the inmates who had need of supplementary scholarly exercises. This inmate was the provincial of the Hungarian Jesuits. Additionally, János' mother sent consecrated hosts (under the form of sweetbread) in the biweekly parcels, which he had the right to receive.

after November 4, the Yugoslavians drove refugees back into Hungary. But, from the moment that the Hungarian authorities went back on their word, arresting the kidnapped Nagy and his companions, Yugoslavia balked, and in reaction, it was again going to admit refugees. Hence, the escape to the south had again become possible. It was simply a matter of getting there.

Feri's fiancée was in Baja and it was decided that the sister of this young girl was going to be my "fiancée." Feri therefore wrote a letter to *his* fiancée about my visit. I put the letter in my pocket, and, travelling by coach and a small train, I reached Kiskunhalas, a city of medium size, known for its lace workshops. When I arrived at Kiskunhalas station, the place wherefrom the train to Baja was going to depart, all the commuters were being led into a large room, and all those who had identity cards mentioning Budapest as the place of residence were being sent back toward the capital. We passed by a sub-officer who inspected our papers, a fellow who came across as rather blinkered. "You have the intention of going where?" "To Baja, to reunite with my fiancée." The sub-officer: "I think that you want to go to Belgrade, not to Baja." I realized that I was virtually done for. The only solution that remained for me was to bluff. So, I turned toward him, and said in an offended tone: "Why do you doubt my words?" The sub-officer lowered his head, chagrined, and indicated that I was henceforth free to take the train for Baja. I knew that I was required to continue the act, so I left very carefully. And sensing his gaze upon my back, I dared to stop myself at the door in order to remark to the soldier guarding it: "This is life; one is always suspected." Indeed, he indicated his approval. I believe that I was the only one freed. All of the others, many hundreds of people, were required to take the train back to Budapest.

That evening, I arrived in Baja to be welcomed by Feri's parents and his fiancée. He knew a man who was a true smuggler, not of merchandise but of people. He told me his name, and explained to me that Mátyás Zomborcsevics lived in a village at the border, wherefrom he came every morning to work in Baja. I was only to meet him upon his arrival at the city's small station. I arrived at the station three minutes late, and the commuters were already marching toward the center of the city. One of them suddenly stopped himself, and, gazing at me with eyes of an extraordinary intensity, said to me: "I shall meet you here tomorrow evening when the train departs." He did not expect to find me, but he had guessed by my appearance that I desired to flee the country. Mátyás was a man of modest origin, speaking Hungarian and Croatian, for his village was binational. During the war, he served in the Hungarian intelligence services. His plane was downed by the Soviets, and he was going to be sentenced to life in prison. He was deported to the Soviet Far East, where he was employed on a seal-hunting boat, which used to leave early each morning. For sustenance, the hunter-prisoners swallowed a large glass of seal oil. And in order to be able to swallow it, they first had to drink a glass of vodka . . . Mátyás was granted amnesty upon the death of Stalin in '53. He was able to return to his hometown, but he decided to avenge himself. He therefore managed to have himself recruited by the Yugoslavian Espionage Service (for he already spoke Croatian and Hungarian, and he had also learnt Russian), being enlisted as an interpreter in the Soviet barracks located within proximity of his village. During the day, he exercised the functions of an interpreter in the barracks; during the night, he drove refugees to the other side of the border.

On the evening of the following day, I arrive at the station. But—misery and misfortune—a large soldier pacing back and forth in front of the edifice said to me: "You want to take the train? Since this morning, the entire region South of Baja has again become 'border district.'" One couldn't go there but with a special permit. So, I decided to continue the bluff: "But, comrade, I've come from afar to meet my fiancée; I cannot retrace my steps . . ." The nice but simple man quickly gave in: "Take the train if you like, but if you are arrested, that will be your own fault . . ." I therefore boarded the train. Frightened, I spot right in front of me two Soviet officers, but they didn't greatly care about the travelers. All of a sudden, I see Mátyás crossing my wagon. I follow him, and he explains to me that there are others, a lady from Budapest with her small son, both of whom he will have to smuggle into Yugoslavia with me. Mrs. D. was an Anglicist at the Budapest university, separated from her husband, a reformed pastor. She was disguised as a peasant girl with a very authentic looking headscarf. Her son was seven years old. She had also brought her five-year-old daughter with her, although Mátyás had said to her: "Madam, I can't take both of your children to Yugoslavia at the same time, but I promise you that I will return as soon as tomorrow to bring the little girl back with me then." Mátyás instantly fell in love with Mrs. D., but he was in any case a man of honor. And indeed, two days later, he arrived in Yugoslavia with the little Sophie, who, throughout the entire night's journey, slept tranquilly on his shoulders . . . Incidentally, that was Mátyás' last return to Hungary. When he went to search for the little Sophie, he learnt that he had been discovered and was on the verge of being arrested by the Soviets. We were going to be together in Yugoslavia during the first part of my "captivity." But when I left him, having been transferred to another camp, I left to him, as a souvenir, the famous piece of Madách: *Tragedy of Man*, written around 1860. Mátyás Zomborcsevics ended up being welcomed into Sweden, wherefrom he would write to me saying that the book I gave him had saved him from madness. Almost fifty years later, I managed to again make contact with him. He had married a Swedish woman, but was very unhappy. According to his rather confusing letters, the Swedes detested the Hungarians, and they suspended, unjustly, his driving license. Perhaps twelve years ago, I received a letter in French from his widow informing me that Mátyás had passed away, and that his funeral service was celebrated by a Catholic priest.

The small train we caught in Baja had arrived at its second and last station, in Gara, the small village where Mátyás lived, and we exited the train together, Mrs. D., her small son, and I. We were following Mátyás, when, all of a sudden, we saw the Hungarian police in front of us. Mrs. D. turned to the left to slip away into a small street, but there she saw two Soviet officers, facing her, marching toward the station. We were terrified. But neither the police nor the officers had noticed us: It was almost dark, and in any case, nothing of interest was ever known to happen in Gara . . . Led by Mátyás, we arrived at a house: that of a peasant, who was a professional smuggler. He however, unlike Mátyás, asked for money. But, as it so happened, the tariff was moderate enough.[16] Mátyás told us to try to sleep, for he would awaken us when we had to leave. He too was rather on edge, drawing circles on the wall with his flashlight. I took a pill to calm myself and quickly fell into sleep. Around five hours later, we are awoken. It is time to depart. It is around three o'clock, a humid night, but not completely black. I am carrying a bag belonging to Mrs. D. Mátyás has András around his neck. (The small boy of seven years had marched courageously at the beginning, but he became too tired to continue on foot.) We hear dogs barking, and Mátyás has us pass through a winding path. He would later tell us that this was to avoid the tents in which Soviet soldiers were sleeping. We walk and walk, and close to six-thirty, Mátyás turns toward us, and says with a smile: "We are on the other side. We are in Yugoslavia." We find ourselves before bales of straw, and, being exhausted, we sit down, or rather fall to the ground.

16. To be a smuggler during this winter was a lucrative profession. I myself almost became one. Still in the month of November, I met, on the streets of Szeged, a couple who lived in the same Budapest building where I used to live with my parents. They were overjoyed to see me but asked whether I could help them cross the border. I said yes, for I knew a smuggler. This smuggler demanded of them a large sum of money, but the couple insisted that, in addition, I accept five hundred florins (which equated to the monthly amount of my scholarship) for myself. They also wanted to give me a packet of condoms. I no longer remember how I explained the reasons that made me refuse this supplementary offer . . . I decided to celebrate the event, so I invited some friends to the famous Virag pastry shop, which had beautiful Biedermeier-styled furniture. We had been offered the establishment's specialty: chestnut cream with whipped cream. Some hours later, I once again found the couple from Budapest. They had returned, unsuccessful, from the proximity around the border, which had become too dangerous. Obviously, I returned their money—deducting, however, fifty florins: the price of our cups of chestnut cream . . .

Perhaps half an hour later, we see Yugoslavian border guards, who led us to the small station of a village, the name of which I have forgotten. Hence, it was over. We had arrived. This was freedom. All of this was true, but during the three-and-a-half months that I would spend in various camps in Yugoslavia, I didn't feel entirely sure. After all, I still found myself in a communist country.[17]

From that village, we were transported to the small city of Zombor. The twenty-five kilometers traveled in ninety minutes represents, in my view, a record of railway slowness (and I used trains in Spain in 1957 and in India thirty years later). Zombor (Sombor in Serbian) was the maternal city of my grandmother who lived in Felcsút. When I learnt that our first destination was going to be Zombor, I thought again of familial history. My grandmother was born in this city, and her grandfather, an officer in the Revolution of '48, József Weisz, was hidden by his Serbian neighbors in a bread-baking oven when the Austrian soldiers had come to arrest him. In fact, he was never going to be arrested. Fifty-five years after this time in Zombor, when speaking to philosophers of the Serbian Academy, I began my talk by recounting that my great grandfather had been saved by the Serbians, just as I was one hundred and seven years later. The majority of the city of Zombor was hungarophone—it was situated to the north of the Province of Vojvodina, which had been reattached to Yugoslavia by the Treaty of Trianon—and we had been accommodated in the Hungarian casino. Mattresses were placed in the vast showroom of the establishment, and I, I believe, slept on a table. We spent fifteen days in Zombor. We didn't have the right to leave, but I did once manage to escape: I was seeking a church, and noted, with astonishment, that the Carmelites still had their church. (In Hungary, almost all the churches belonging to monastic orders had been either closed or changed into diocesan churches.) In our group of rather disparate refugees was a very dignified old peasant woman with her three girls. She was a Jehovah's Witness, and guarded, as if it were some precious treasure, a notebook in which prophecies had been laid onto paper. The end of the world was predicted from the appearance of Hitler, who was the Beast of the Apocalypse. The text must have been written in the early Forties, and when the death of Hitler wasn't followed by the end of the world, someone had crossed out the name of Hitler to replace it with that of Eisenhower! The elderly lady asked me from time to time to read her passages of the Bible, because I had, it seems, a very beautiful voice. One day after the scriptural

17. For my time in Yugoslavia, see the interview that I gave to M. Losoncz ("A gyógyulást az jelentette, amikor az álom elmaradt . . . [The Healing had been Signified by the Disappearance of the Dreams . . .]," 146–56), and my aforementioned reflection ("Miklós, You Should Change Your Ideology," 144–7).

reading, she looks at me and says: "You are a good and pious person; how is it that you come to adore idols?" This was evidently about the saints and the Virgin Mary. I tried to explain that the Catholic cult of the saints wasn't idolatry but simply to request their intercession. She wasn't convinced. To her defense, it must be said that she probably had Catholic neighbors, who, like Grandma's maid, Julis, believed that Saint Elizabeth of Hungary resided in the corner of the Moon. The elderly lady wanted to go to Jerusalem to be in the Holy City when the end of the world arrives. Her daughters said to her: "Okay, but let's first pass through the United States."

During these fifteen days in Zombor, I managed to mail a postcard to my parents. But I wasn't going to hear any news from them for still quite a while. From Zombor, we were transported by train to a refugee camp further to the south. We changed trains at Belgrade, and by an extraordinary stroke of luck, at the station I would meet Dr. Gondos and his family, all of whom were on their way to Germany after having spent some weeks in a Yugoslavian refugee camp. Of Belgrade, I didn't see much. A Hungarian student had once heard us speak. He came to see us, but he was also afraid of being seen by the police while he spoke with our group. We had been driven to Neresnica, a lost town in the municipality of Kučevo, to the south-east of Belgrade. I no longer know how we had settled. I simply remember having decided to wash myself in the stream that ran along the camp. The water must have been around four degrees. I preferred to get out of it as swiftly as possible . . . Neresnica was the end of the world, as was all of Serbia—a country occupied by Turks for almost four centuries. In the streets of the village, we saw Orthodox priests with strange head-coverings and some kind of oriental slippers on their feet. We visited—I know neither how nor why—a family. In their home, there was no furniture except for one bed for the father and the two sons, and another for the mother and the two daughters, plus a rope to dry the laundry.

We also began to receive mail, and I remember one letter from my father, which, with much justice, made me aware that he wasn't ignorant of the difficulties of the life I had to lead, but neither did he, being a former prisoner of the SS, find it necessary for me to exaggerate my complaints. I also received linen—of a very poor quality[18]—and money from my family in Israel. In fact, they were themselves very poor, even six years after their emigration there. But that, I didn't know. As far as I knew, all those who were living outside communist countries had to be comfortable people.[19]

18. I left Hungary with a missal, a French dictionary, and some volumes of poetry, but as for clothes, only that which I had on my back. When my only shirt was drying, I was in a sweater . . .

19. I was going to be subjected to the same behavior four months later, when,

We had been correctly treated in this camp, yet I protested. I created an uproar, and I was finally taken before the commandant of the camp, a colonel of some fifty years of age. I was courageous—or rather, insolent—and I began to lose my temper. He listened to me for a few moments. Then he approached me. He seized me by the neck, and pushed me out of his office. Reflecting upon the situation, I recognize that he wasn't in the wrong.

Having shown my insolent behavior, I was sent to another camp, located in Croatia, some four hundred and fifty kilometers away from Neresnica. Gerovo was an old farming village, and we were lodged in a long building, formerly a bull stable. Thus, I signed and dated my letters from Gerovo, Bull Hotel . . . We slept and dwelled with roughly one hundred of us in an enormous room. We were rather poorly nourished, and I remember having one day received a parcel containing smoked meats coming from Apatin on the Tisza. The sender was a certain H. L., a maker of musical instruments, and a cousin of my friend Ferenc Kiefer. (The Kiefers were originally from this small town of Vojvodina, which was, like Zombor, formerly Hungarian.) Hence, I decided to organize a feast. And, with the company of three friends, we devoured, in a single effort, the entire contents of this package. Among the refugees, we also had a priest who celebrated Mass for us (my first in some two months) and lent me piety books (even though they were, alas, extraordinarily shallow) . . . I also made the acquaintance of a Franciscan brother whom I was again going to meet in Paris. Incidentally, he had quickly left the habit—a decision motivated by, among other things, the fact that in France, priests and the faithful didn't correctly pronounce Latin, that is to say, according to the vigorous pronunciation in the countries of Central Europe . . . We didn't have much to do, so we prepared crossword puzzles. A group of four prisoners presented us with crosswords, which, with the help of a friend—an orthopedist, who was going to make his career in Cleveland—we quickly deciphered. Then, it was our turn to craft the puzzles. But we decided to play a trick upon the four fellows. We drew an immense rectangle of one hundred by one hundred and twenty lines. The first eight were sensible, but thereafter we designed the content to be deciphered as "brother-in-law in Patagonia" or "carrots in the past" or the like. The four chaps spent days attempting to finish the puzzle. They had made a copy of the rectangle, the original being covered by pencil marks. When they understood that they had been had, the orthopedist said to me: "I did judo when I was a student. It would, however, be better for you to disappear!"

---

hardly having arrived in Paris, I receive an almost illegible letter from Uncle Charles, the nearly-nonagenarian brother of my maternal grandfather, asking me to send him worn out vestments.

Time was passing, but I still found myself in communist Yugoslavia, and I had since the beginning been aiming for France. Thanks to family acquaintances living in France, my application for a French visa had been treated relatively quickly, and I knew that I would leave in the near enough future. Without a doubt, the wait was not easy. I had met agreeable people, but also those who were rather lamentable. I remember well one Ernö, a government official of thirty-eight years, a pious and cultivated man. He told me that, during the siege of Budapest, he was made a prisoner by the Russians and was in danger of being sent to Siberia. In his youth, he had received a kind of medical training, so he declared himself a doctor in order to accordingly receive better treatment. He was prescribing aspirin and inhalations, but one day he received a visit from a woman, a Soviet officer in a state of profound despair, confessing to him that she was pregnant and asking him for an abortion. Ernö was a Catholic, and he was not a doctor . . . I also met former political prisoners from the Rákosi epoch, often deep and generous people. But some of the people we had to deal with were very different. A family, for example, feared that one day they wouldn't have enough to eat, so they managed—I don't know how—to have their rations doubled, which they hid under their beds. When they had been transferred to another camp, we found, under their beds, kilos upon kilos of moldy bread. Moreover, good old Hungarian antisemitism had been given over to its heart's content: a red-haired boy with very pronounced Jewish features had been one object of derision. They did not however know my origins. I did have a missal, but all the same, one never knew . . . In any case, the young city-dweller, incapable of drawing water from a deep well, nor knowing how to handle a saw, found little esteem among these people of the country, these clerks, these ex-military men. The situation was only going to change on the day that, during the distribution of mail, I was called to receive money (sent by my uncle in Israel). From this moment, I was respected.[20] I was also solicited to write letters in French, and most of the time I received precise and detailed instructions. For example, a family of farmers who wanted to obtain Canadian visas handed me the rough draft of a letter: "Mister Ambassador! We arrived in Neresnica . . ." Another family wanted to reconnect with an uncle who had emigrated to Cleveland, and yet for twenty years

20. In any case, I was considered opulent. We had rations of cigarettes, which the very small number of non-smokers used to cede to the others in exchange for money. I, however, didn't see what could be done with money in Neresnica, so I simply gifted my cigarettes to my comrades. But I do remember once having used a part of my ration to press my demand of a boy skilled at woodcutting to make a doll for Sophie, the daughter of Mrs. D. Toys were not provided in the Yugoslavian camps.

hadn't given them any sign of life. The letter addressed to this uncle had to open with the ritual phrase:

"Dear Uncle Joseph,

Thank you for your letter. As for us, we are going well . . ."

After some five weeks in Gerovo, I ended up being informed of the fact that my French visa had arrived, and that while awaiting departure to France, I was going to be transferred to one last camp. To get there, we needed to pass through Zagreb, where I was housed in a Red Cross center. I spent four days at this center. In fact, I was always leaving to stroll through the city. One day, I return to find the headmistress waiting for me in order to hurl invective at me. "Where were you? A soldier came to escort you to another camp." "Madam, I was at Mass." It was Communism, but she was, despite everything else, a Croatian woman! Other than myself, there were mainly middle-aged women who didn't have much to do. I went to the laundry to do my washing, I confess, with the hope that someone wouldn't let me do it, because I didn't have any idea how it was to be done. As it so happened, the women saw me going about this business. "What are you doing there? You have no idea how to wash clothes. Go on, get out of here . . . We'll wash your things." I obeyed, with very little protest . . . A more sordid story: Among the residents of the Red Cross center, there was a young woman. During lunch, she began to speak of her husband, who she said did not understand her. "I had never before cheated on him, but then I decided to do it." I managed to excuse myself, but I saw her a little later in the company of a muscular and unsympathetic fellow who certainly understood her.

At the end of the four days, a policeman had presented himself to escort me. While waiting in the station's refreshment room, he wanted to order me a beer. "No thank you; I don't drink." Then he offers me a cigarette. "Thank you, but I don't smoke." "So what do you live for then?" He led me to Stubičke Toplice, a popular waterside resort near Zagreb. (Forty-seven years later, I gave directions to two Croatian girls at the Kyoto station, and one of the two knew this vacation spot very well.) Of course, we were lodged six to a room, but what was marvelous was the pool . . . As for the other refugees, they were, I think, all people who had to leave for France. A lady was there with her twenty-year-old son, the same age as me. I don't know why, but she and the son took a disliking toward me, behaving truly odiously. I was however able to have my revenge when we were in France at the Montbéliard refugee camp and Mrs. X, who didn't know French, was trying to be understood in German, without success. I therefore asked her very politely: "*Can I help you?*" She was furious, but it was quite necessary that she accept my services. Among the people at this last station of my life as a refugee, I remember two couples, relatively aged. Mister M. was a former professor of

Franciscan theology. Although a defrocked priest, he continued to profess his Catholic orthodoxy. Thirty-five years later, I met his son at a convention, where he taught me that his father had again undertaken the service of a minister, but this time as an Episcopalian priest . . . The other couple, Mister S. and his wife, loved me with veritable parental affection. He was twenty-four years senior to his wife. She was very kind, very nice, but poorly understood my manner of living. One day, she said to me: "It's your fiancée, not you, who should arrive at the altar dressed in white for your marriage!" He however was goodness, correctness, piousness. In Paris, he was going to work in a company on the other side of the city, and he would say his rosary during the fifty minutes of metro travel back and forth. Unfortunately, like many refugees, being unable to adapt to the country that had welcomed them, they would only think about leaving, and dreamt of emigrating to America. They didn't know French, but instead of trying to learn it, they hurriedly studied English grammar. They were able to attend our engagement Mass, and after it they told me how "fine" they found Odile's family. Mrs. S. died very young, at forty-seven years of age. But he was going to die much later, aged eighty-eight, leaving the memory of a good, noble, tender man. I was able to see him again two years before his death.[21]

21. I remember an extraordinary scene only a short while after our arrival in Paris: I had gone with Mister S. to a post office in order to help him telephone his nonagenarian mother in Hungary. The post office employees—and not only them—were deeply moved to see this man with white hair, approaching his seventieth year, in tears while talking to his mother.

Grandparents' house, Felcsút (1920?)

Mrs. János Vető, Éva Aczél (1907–1945), mother of Miklós Vető

János Vető (1901–1941), father of Miklós Vető

Miklós Vető, Felcsút (1938/9?)

With Mrs. Miklós Vető, Anna Sabel (1898–1964),
adoptive mother, Felcsút (1941?)

With his brother, István Vető (1938–1948?)

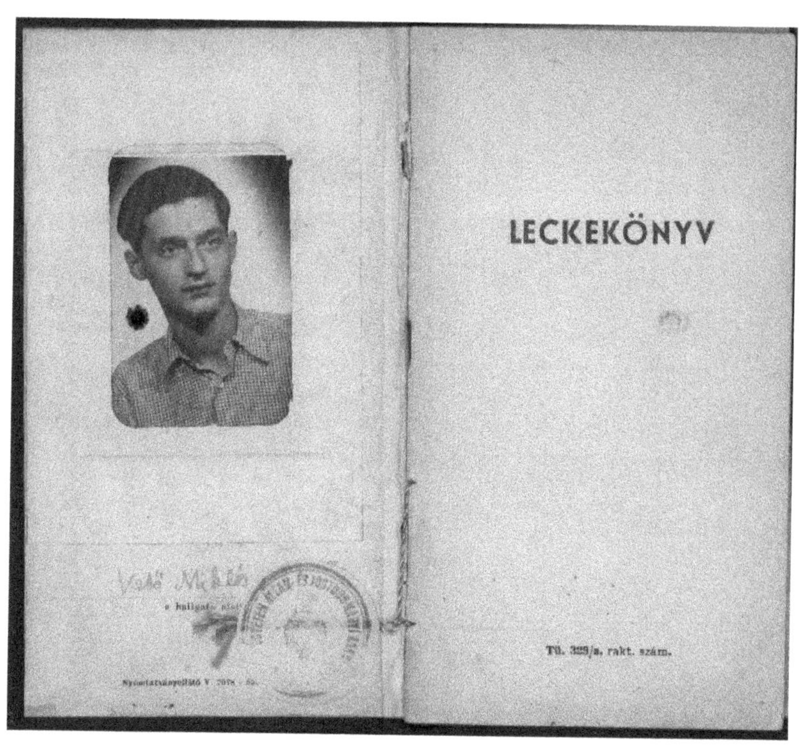

Photo in the book of the Law Faculty of the University of Szeged (September 1954)

Miklós Vető at the general assembly of the MEFESZ in Szeged (October 20, 1956)
© Móra Ferenc Museum, Szeged

Postface

Sixty Years Later

1.

With the arrival in Montbéliard had commenced a new period of my life. And this period has so far accounted for sixty-two years in the life of the octogenarian that I now am. What is new and what is old in this life? Does it suffer radical discontinuities, or does it only unfold, bring to fruition, that which was already there from the very start, that which took form in childhood and adolescence, that which the young man of twenty years felt and thought, was and wanted? The answer is that continuity and discontinuity are here indissociable, that they constitute the tissue of my life, that they define and determine that which I am on the basis of that which I was, and perhaps announce and prefigure that which I will be. As a fervent reader of Kant, I never ceased meditating upon the famous teaching in the *Critique* on the "thing-in-itself" and the "appearance." This theory, this discourse on the entire world must also guide my self-interpretation. The thing-in-itself is the ground, the foundation, the core of a being. The appearance, however, is the translation of this foundation in space and time. That which I have been has been given to me, starting from my conception, and it is this self which, through its conscious and unconscious moments, exists, progresses, and is structured. Like one's fingerprint, one's very being is singular and unique, even if it does not cease moving through events and actions which seem, if not to destroy one's identity, then at least to render it knowable only with difficulty. The life of each one of us is a unique figure, deployed in its own manner. This deployment is driven and articulated by the incessant synthesis of the continuous with the discontinuous, of the old which survives with the new that arrives. In that which concerns me, the new is the story of my life in different countries, of studies and work at various universities, and of philosophy, which is my profession—a profession which fills my life, and which gives me a frame of reference to understand things. The new also includes my family, the spouse whom I met near the start of my life in the West, with whom I've had children, and grandchildren, also a great grandchild on the way. And yet the family is an example *par excellence* of the fact that the old and the new cannot be dissociated. When I married Odile, I had entered into her family, but I also kept mine. With the passing of years, parents disappear, but in marriages new parents are born. And this fecund interweaving of the old and the new is equally seen in the identities that emerge from my roots: in my Hungarian identity, and my Jewish identity. For sixty-two years, with an interruption between 1959 and 1979, I have lived in France. I love France, and I would not like to leave it, but I am not French. I was born Hungarian, and that is what I remain. Indeed, I continue to feel this belonging to Hungary ever more strongly, even if I would not like to return to live in the country of my birth. As for my Jewish identity, it is essentially familial, it is of blood. One could even say that it is racial, not truly religious. It is a hidden identity that one endures, so to say, despite oneself, but from which one cannot be liberated. Personally, I also try to assume it, and to understand it through the essential belonging to the Church, which nourishes my Christian faith. I can enumerate decisive moments and events of my life, moments and events which express and betray who I am, moments and events which have opened me up to new avenues, or which have permitted me to better march through the old ones. But no other moments or events ever had the decisive significance of those few foundational seconds in the February of 1954, while crossing the boulevard near our apartment in Budapest. They sent me to the Church in which I have been ever since, in which I live, and in which I live happily. The Catholic, Christian faith, which I share with those close to me, is the force which makes me be and act, which inspires and articulates my thought, which constitutes the strongest identity of my life. I do not know what is reserved for me in the years that remain, but I know that it is faith in Jesus Christ which allows me to live in joy.

2.

FROM MONTBÉLIARD, MY FIRST place of residence in France, I took the train for Paris to go to the office that handled Hungarian student refugees. We numbered some six hundred in France; yet we obtained, each one of us, a government grant. The social services assistant began explaining to me that I was in fact going to receive a grant, but that I had to leave to do my studies at the University of Caen, that of Paris being overloaded. Since my childhood, I had dreamt of Paris, the center of French civilization, the city of painters and poets. I therefore replied to the kind lady that I had not taken part in the Revolution in order to live in the provinces. She said to me, smiling, that this was fine, but that I had eight days to find lodging, otherwise it would be well and truly necessary for me to go to Caen. I ended up quickly finding accommodation. First, I lived in a miserable maid's room on the seventh story of an old house. It was a miniscule hole, and without running water. Four weeks later, I succeeded in moving to the home of an elderly lady. There, I was going to enjoy a large room in a comfortable, almost elegant building. The only problem was the bathroom. The apartment had one of them, spacious and in good condition. However, the bath—of which the faucets functioned perfectly—was unusable, and this for the good reason that it only served to accommodate a large heap of coal . . .[22]

22. I made the acquaintance of many people, those young as well as those less young, during my student years in Paris. I would only like to mention, outside of my academic masters, Jean Letourneau. I met the former minister and Governor General of Indochina at a Eucharistic congress in Sarthe, where I'd gone fourteen days after my arrival in Paris to present a testimony about my life. I was thereafter frequently invited to the Letourneaus' apartment in Paris. And this would permit me to have the experience of a little contemporary history: One day, I ask Madeleine, the eldest of the three young Letourneau daughters: "From where comes this beautiful alabaster statue that you have in your office?" "It is of Emperor Bao Daï of Vietnam; he offered it to me when I obtained my high school diploma . . ." A dozen years later, during a lunch at the Letourneau home, I found myself sitting in front of Georges Bidault, one of the former and most important government leaders of the Fourth Republic. Mister Bidault, very reactionary, was in the process of inveighing against the reforms of the Second Vatican Council, and he expressed his fears that the Catholic Church would admit the marriage of priests. I was and still am firmly convinced of the importance of priestly celibacy. But even though the immense majority of Catholic priests, those of the *Latin* rite, must not marry, the Catholic priests of the *Eastern* rite can marry *before* their ordination, even if their bishops are only chosen from among the priests who have remained celibate. So, I was unable to resist saying to Georges Bidault: "Mister President, what would you say if you were a Catholic priest of the Greek rite, and married?" And Bidault turned toward me: "I would say to myself, my friend, that I will never be bishop!"

I waited impatiently for the recommencement of university, which took place at the beginning of November. I was admitted into second year philosophy studies. We had famous professors such as Vladimir Jankélévitch and Raymond Aron, and I also attended for almost an entire semester the marvelous patristic course by the future Cardinal Daniélou at the Catholic Institute. Of all these masters to whom I listened, it was however Claude Lévi-Strauss whom I found the most fascinating. The author of *Tristes Tropiques* spoke to an audience mainly composed of people much older than me: specialists in philosophy and researchers in sociology and ethnology. Lévi-Strauss brought with him, as early as his first lesson, a small carved Indian comb, and for the whole year, starting from the analysis of sculptures, he was going to explain and meticulously dissect the social structures of the tribe that had fabricated this comb. I used to seat myself in a corner at the back of the room, and one day, between classes, I gathered my courage with both hands and went to see the master: "Professor, could you please give me an introductory bibliography on the mythology of the Indians of North America?" And Lévi-Strauss responds with an unpleasant smile: "Young man, there exists no introductory bibliography." I went to fold myself up again, without pronouncing a word, back into the cubbyhole that was my corner of the room . . .

I was doing well enough with my exams at the Sorbonne, but I knew perfectly well that I had to quickly leave. I would have wanted to obtain an academic teaching position. But teachers were civil servants, and to be a civil servant, it was necessary to be French. One becomes French on completion of a five-year process at minimum, but during these five years, it is necessary to earn a living. But, to earn a living, it is necessary to be a civil servant, and to be a civil servant, one had to be French! In any case, I was pressed: My adoptive parents were elderly, my lawyer father couldn't earn a living in communist Hungary, and he was quickly going to retire. This is to say that I was going to have to help them. Hence, I had to work. In the Fifties and Sixties (even much later too by the way), this kind of situation could be solved by obtaining a post in a higher education institution in the United States. And the royal road to get there passed through a renowned English university. Hence, I decided to go to Oxford. However, I didn't know English, nor did I have any scholarship to undertake studies in England. I therefore began to take English classes, and I picked up a small French scholarship for eight months of study in England.

I arrived in Oxford at the beginning of November 1959. At the recommendation of Jean Wahl, I had gone to see the celebrated Isaiah Berlin, one of the great political thinkers of the 20th century, and a very important personality at Oxford. Berlin would effectively help me find a four-year thesis scholarship. My financial bases were therefore assured, but I found myself in a world very different from all that I had until then known. The University of Oxford is composed of a certain number of "colleges," of which a great many have medieval origins. As for mine, Saint Antony's, it was one of the most recent. It was founded by a French explorer, one who was suspected of all kinds of trafficking in Africa and the Arabian Peninsula, including slave trading. The *college* had a majority of foreign students served by *scouts*, English domestic servants. The bathrooms functioned correctly. A nice park was located behind the central edifice. And we didn't cease to welcome illustrious visitors. I once found myself at a reception beside Sir Harald McMillan, who had just finished his mandate as Prime Minister. And one day at breakfast, I was seated facing Alexander Kerensky himself, the last head of the Russian Government before the Communist Revolution of October.

Oxford was a town full of magnificent, ancient edifices, of medieval or classical style. Its inhabitants, courteous and proper. But they were in large majority English, and the English are different—different from the French, different from the Hungarians, different from the Europeans—in fact, different *as such*. And the philosophy that I was going to have to study was also very different from all that I had known until then. I myself was impassioned by metaphysics while *Oxford Philosophy* was essentially an analysis of words and expressions. But I ended up finding a thesis supervisor closer to my own manner of thinking. Iris Murdoch was a great novelist and a good practitioner of moral philosophy. She had accepted me for work on Simone Weil, and during our first personal encounter, she asked me to give her a *bibliography* on this great French thinker . . .[23] The thesis permitted me to apply for a place in the American higher education system, and I ended up being recruited to Marquette University. Odile and I were already married, and she too was able to obtain a position at Marquette.[24]

23. I had just been invited to deliver a talk at the great conference that will take place at Oxford in 2019, on the occasion of the hundredth birthday of Iris Murdoch.

24. I met Odile in 1958 at the Richelieu Center. We hardly saw each other for some time thereafter, but when I returned from Oxford in May 1960 to defend my M.A., and she, from Florence to defend her own, we found each other again by pure chance, but this time in front of the Sorbonne. When she had learnt that the boat which brought me from England back to France arrived at Dieppe, she said to me: "We live in Neufchâtel-en-Bray, not far from Dieppe. When you next return to France, stop by our home." I didn't know any family from the provinces, so I said to myself: "From a sociological point of view, it could be interesting to make the acquaintance of the Wattré family." Some six weeks later, I was indeed going to arrive at their home. After dinner, I took, with Odile, a long stroll, and I spoke with her about my life. The following day, we caught the train that brought us to the Council (the end of year assembly) at the Richelieu Center. But then I had to leave Paris for Vienna to undertake German classes. In making my farewell, I said to Odile: "I would be happy to find a *letter* awaiting me." She

Marquette is located in Milwaukee, along the border of Lake Michigan. It is in the Midwest, Middle America, where these two young doctors, totaling fifty-four years between them, landed at the start of September 1963. Marquette was one of the United States' best Catholic universities, a university in which philosophy played an important role. It was actually scholastic philosophy that all of my colleagues, with exception only to one, fervently practiced. But this was the age of the Second Vatican Council. One spoke of openness, and it was the desire for this openness that had permitted the recruiting of someone who had written a thesis on Simone Weil and had also begun to develop an interest in Schelling. I was happy to teach, even if the majority of my students were in all honesty very mediocre. And during these two years, I was also able to write some articles. But we had always considered the Milwaukee institution to be an initial position, something temporary, and at the end of our second year at Marquette, we were able to move on, for I had been recruited to Yale.

Yale . . . It is one of the great American universities. There, I found myself among brilliant colleagues and before magnificent students. One of these students has since become one of the most important Jewish theologians in America. Another left in her third year of philosophy for China, wherefrom she returned with an 18th century map in order to prepare a critical edition. A third defended a superb and substantial dissertation on Nietzsche. I had lost track of him for forty odd years, only to recently reunite with him in a Paris metro of all places. I was seated beside a lady who was reading a translation of one of the recent novels by Samuel Savage . . . In addition to brilliant colleagues and magnificent students, I also had at my disposal one of the largest libraries in the world: the famous *Sterling Library*. It possesses almost all that has been published in the different Western languages, and to furnish the bibliography of a scholarly work, it sufficed—or at least almost so—to consult the Sterling catalogue. But, rather unfortunately, Yale was found in America, and I myself wanted to live in France, to teach at a French university. However, the rules of public service in France had barely changed since my departure for Oxford: To be recruited to a faculty position, it was necessary to be French. So, I undertook the required steps, and I was received by a minister of de Gaulle, who—with an extraordinary letter of recommendation from the great philosopher Gabriel Marcel[25] in my folio—would do what was necessary. For me, the Council of State was going to apply an article of exception from the code of French nationality:

had heard, due to my accent, "a *being* [être]" instead of "a *letter* [lettre]," but she well understood what I wanted to say to her. We were engaged a short while later.

25. I dedicated one of my last books to Marcelian thought. [See *Gabriel Marcel* in the bibliography.]

this being that a foreigner who has rendered, or is capable of rendering, exceptional services to France, can be naturalized without delay. I later learnt that this article is mostly used for spies, who had to be urgently repatriated.

I was therefore naturalized as a French citizen, and I undertook a tour of the universities in metropolitan France in order to search for work. I had been politely welcomed practically everywhere, but I hadn't found anything. Either there hadn't been a vacant post, or there had been one, but there was a local candidate who had to be considered before everyone else. I had been naturalized in 1970, during a sabbatical year in France, but I would still be in America and without a French post in 1975. Fortunately, we ended up finding a solution. The universities of the African francophone states most often had as their professors French teachers who, after some years of service, found, either for the first time or once again, a post in the metropolis. I was therefore accepted to the National University of the Ivory Coast in Abidjan, where we were going to spend four helpful and pleasant years. To be sure, most of my French colleagues weren't of very high class, but I had numerous good students who demonstrated a touching fidelity. I'm still in contact with many of them. And, thirty-five years after our return to France, I was invited back to Abidjan to receive the National Order of Merit, and a superb gown worn by the Elder of the Yakouba people, a member of whom had written, under my direction, a good thesis on Kant's political philosophy.

We were happy in Abidjan. But the climate, geographic and moral, of an African country was not very favorable to the writing of works of erudition or philosophical speculation. And above all, I aspired to return with my family to France, and obtain an academic post there. After many attempts, steps, and moves, I was finally named a university professor in France. A dream—a dream of almost twenty years—was realized. I had become a university professor, and I was going to remain one until my retirement in 2005. From 1979 until 1993, I lectured at Rennes, and from 1993 until 2005, the year of my retirement, I was going to teach at Poitiers. I would have rather liked in the meantime to pass through the Sorbonne. I regret not having been recruited there, and what's worst is that I can't even complain. I would have been able to denounce the injustice if someone of less worth than I had been preferred. Alas, quite unfortunately, it was my friend Jean-François Marquet who had been taken—the only candidate who I had to consider as better than me! The twenty-six years in faculty would leave a mitigated memory. I had much time for my own work, and the basis of this work was the writing of articles and books. However, I noted with a sad impotence the limits of my teaching work. I prepared my courses with very great care, and I don't think that my students were ever bored. But, unfortunately, the French university system favored barely any contact between professors and students. The lecture is only the peak of a structure in which student and teacher barely encountered each other personally. On the other hand, the ever-tightening grip of the preparatory classes upon the truly talented youths inevitably empties the classrooms of the best students. Without a doubt, I was never discouraged from preparing my lessons by the mediocrity, nay, feebleness of my students. But I am saddened to have to confess that, in composing a list of friends and disciples based on the students whom I've had over the period of fifty years, I've only had one from among them who's worked with me in a French university. As said by one of the former presidents of the University of Rennes I: "The particularity of a French university is that it makes the best, the strongest teachers, lecture before the most mediocre, the weakest students."

3.

We had arrived in France in 1979, and we knew that it was for good. Odile was born French. The children, with the exception of Étienne, were more or less French. And me, well, I had links to this country, very different to all those which I was able to have with the other countries in which I had lived. But, this consciousness, this certitude of being in France "for good," in no sense prevented me from sojourning in other countries. I had lived for twenty years in Hungary without being able to travel, and it was quite necessary to "catch up with" what I wasn't able to do during that time. In fact, if I have a passion in life beside philosophy, it's travel, and this, for two reasons. On the one hand, I'm still crazy about the fine arts, and my voyages are punctuated by incessant visits to museums and monuments. On the other hand, I'm fascinated and attracted by that which is foreign, that which is unknown, and travel—from transitory stops lasting only a few days to stays of several months—is the way *par excellence* to experience the unknown. I have hitherto visited almost sixty countries across the five continents. The shortest voyages were centered around visits to museums and monuments, even if they were often connected to delivering lectures or participating in conferences. Among these short voyages, those to ex-communist countries had a particular taste and significance. I recall one lunch during 1984 in Prague, one of the great cities of the Austro-Hungarian Empire. I was with an unknown Czech who suddenly turned toward me to ask: "Why did you"—meaning the Westerners—"stop in May 1945, why didn't you enter our country *before* the Soviets to save us from subjugation to Communism?" I recall a voyage by train in Transylvania, which I had wanted to take during the night in order to avoid seeing the towns and rivers that were formerly Hungarian. I was, however, awoken with a jolt close to midnight when the train stopped at a small station: that of the city in which S. Petöfi, the emblematic poet of revolutionary Hungary, had fallen during battle in 1849. I've gone many times to tiny Lithuania—first while it was still Soviet, then, independent—where I didn't encounter anyone who wouldn't have had family members, or themselves, deported deep into Russia, to Siberia. As for Poland, I came to know of it while still in France, through a young engaged couple whom the state of war, declared in 1981, had prevented from returning home. These youngsters wanted to marry and had asked us to prepare them for marriage. But they didn't seem overly interested. We said to ourselves: "These are traditional old-fashioned Catholics." But a few days before their marriage, they showed us a paper of the archdiocese of Warsaw certifying that they had participated in thirty-two marriage preparation classes! And once, in Poland itself, an academic colleague from Kraków recounted to me the story of his conversion. He was an atheist, but during the state of war, people could only be reunited in the churches, and the Real Presence of Christ in the Sacrament of the Alter was irresistible. Another memory is that of the Warsaw station. Having arrived there on a Sunday at half past five in the morning, while waiting to be able to get out into the city, I couldn't but put myself to work. However, it became impossible for me to continue come six o'clock, for the loudspeakers began to air Mass, and this continued throughout the entire morning, all while being communist Poland! Finally, in the small Subcarpathian Ukraine, among a minority of Hungarians and Uniates, I was going to find myself in the city where the young archbishop had been murdered in 1947. His car had been overturned by a truck of the Secret Police, but he had survived and was in the process of recovering. Thus, a nurse was sent to his hospital to administer him a lethal injection. Of course, he did not receive a public burial, and it was one of my friends, L. P., a Uniate priest, an excellent painter of icons and a mosaicist, who had found the remains under the edifice which formerly housed the Secret Police.

Another country to which I feel myself close, and not only for touristic reasons, is Israel. It is the country of the Bible, the country of Jesus Christ. And I of course went there many times on pilgrimage, or on voyages interspersed with days of pilgrimage to Jerusalem, to Nazareth, at the edge of the Sea of Galilee. But Israel is not only the country of Jesus Christ and his apostles. It is also the country of the people of modern Israel, where a part of my family lives: Zionists, emigrated after 1945 to what was Palestine under British domination. It is there that I met for the last time my grandmother, who would pass away a few months before her hundredth birthday. It is there that I encountered on the train a Hungarian Jew who formerly lived in the Carpathians, a former wood merchant of his condition, who had assured me that the quality of Israeli wood is nothing beside that of the trees in the Carpathian forests. It is also there that I saw young African students crying on the night of Christmas in Nazareth because Arab teenagers were throwing stones at them.

These sad memories barely accompany the trips that I have made, that we have made, to a great number of very diverse countries. Mexico, Guatemala, and Honduras return to my mind under the sign of the sumptuous Mayan monuments. The palaces of Uxmal, the pyramids of Tikal: these are among the most beautiful things that we have ever seen. And how could we forget the moment when we realized that the noises reaching us from the tops of the trees were emanating from monkeys, when we saw a puma disappear into the scrubland? How could we forget the barefooted Indians visiting the national museum of Guatemala with an enormous parrot perched atop one shoulder, or the distinguished lady who managed a small hotel at the edge of Lake Atitlán, also in Guatemala, explaining that her grandson called himself Vladimiro because his father had read him Dostoyevsky. Also in Guatemala, during our first major trip, we were waiting for the coach in a small provincial town, and the teenager beside us, learning that we were French, cried out "Victor Hugo!" Some thirty-five years later, having the same realization, an Egyptian child enunciated the name "Zidane," the famous football player. A colleague at Yale one day said to me that at the height of these archaeological visits were the Mayans and the Khmers. And, of course, only the temples of Cambodia can be compared to the splendor of the Mayan edifices. However, if, from time to time, we were distressed at the sight of the poverty in Honduras or Guatemala, this was nothing beside the horrors of the Khmer Rouge. Each family that we met had lost many of its members during the dark years of its reign, and even thirty years after the fall of Pol Pot, numerous were the sites unable to be visited because riddled with undetected bombs.

Beside these distant, eccentric lands, we also made visits of a more traditional kind. For our honeymoon, we went to Spain for six weeks, and we couldn't enumerate the shorter or longer stays that we've been able to have in Italy. From Holland, we especially treasure the memory of Rembrandt's flowers; from Iceland, that of the glaciers filling the horizon. From Saint Petersburg, what mainly remains with me is the image, or rather the images, of the Hermitage. In Senegal, I was able to meditate in the port of Gorée, wherefrom slaves were sent to America. From Burkina Faso, it is a boat ride which emerges before my eyes: We saw nothing but birds that seemed to move about, without themselves moving, upon the surface of the lake. They had placed themselves upon the backs of submerged hippopotami, which were swimming ceaselessly. At Rosario in Argentina, the museums were closed on Wednesdays, but an important political man, a candidate for the Vice Presidency of the Republic, had the greatest museum in the city opened for me, with its succession of rooms containing a fantastic quantity of silver plates and dishes. In Chile, the cacti grew in the middle of the snow in the Andes, and the sunset over Valparaíso was enchanting. But we were there during the Pinochet regime, and there were many people in the prisons. In the south of Tunisia, we were able to have an escapade in the desert, just like another that we would have a little later in Dubai, where our children would live. And the collapse of the Soviet Union would allow us trips to the Baltic countries. In Riga in Latvia, we could still ask for information in German, and I remember one medical doctor, embarrassed to learn from me, a foreigner, that it is in Riga itself that the first edition of the *Critique of Pure Reason* was printed. A little further to the north, in Tallinn in Estonia, I was going to have lunch in an elegant restaurant with the Ambassador of France. We were in the process of consuming, sadly, a lamentable meal, which M. F. had tried to improve by ordering a bottle of Beaujolais. Twenty years later, I found myself in Auckland, and knowing that New Zealand is the country of sheep, I asked for a leg of lamb. It came to me boiled . . . I've not been able to visit China, but I was able to deliver a lecture in Hong Kong, a strange city wherein the inhabiting Chinese crowds have, in an incomprehensible manner, the air of Europeans. From Hong Kong, I was able to go to Macau, with its immense gambling casinos and Portuguese baroque churches. I also went to Taipei, in Taiwan, which to me appeared to be a true piece of China, with its National Museum, formerly in Beijing, and its gigantic monument in memory of Chiang Kai-shek. However, the most important voyage to East Asia was going to be the one which brought us to Japan, where I was invited on the occasion of the appearance of a translation of one of my books. We had but fifteen days in this fabulous archipelago, but it was enough to be struck by the kindness and politeness of the people, notably the inhabitants of Kyoto and Tokyo, who bend themselves over backward in order to help you. While in Japan, I had to deliver several lectures. But we had also been invited to a traditional high-end restaurant, where people ate while sitting on their heels. We were, fortunately, exempted from this obligation. The Japanese seemed to me perhaps even more different to the rest of humanity than the English. It was therefore only stranger to suddenly discover, at the site of the giant Buddha of Kamakura, a Hungarian delegation, which Odile had recognized from afar by seeing the solid moustaches that each one sported.

The trips of which I've spoken up to this point were often fascinating, but, with the exception of the one to Spain for our honeymoon, none of them lasted more than fifteen days. There was however one country in which I only travelled and delivered lectures, and this, over two periods, each one lasting around thirty days. This was the marvelous, the magnificent India, which I roamed from north to south. The first time, I began to lose patience at an international congress in New Delhi, when, right in the middle of the Afghanistan War, the personalities representing the communist and third-world countries denounced the American "imperialists" as enemies of peace. Before the stupefied silence of various collaborators and sympathizers of the Soviet Union, I explained that, at that very moment, there was but one true war in the world, and that was the one which the Red Army was waging in Afghanistan. As for my second adventure, it would come to an end in Pondicherry, a tropical city, with its cathedral constructed under Louis XVI. During these two long trips, separated in time by two years, I visited the marvels of India and didn't stop addressing audiences of students and researchers, brimming with good will even if not extremely adept. I was able to rest for some days in Varanasi, Mumbai, and Tiruchirappalli, but the most beautiful memories are of the Taj Mahal of Agra, the Jain temples of Ranakpur, and the caves of Ajanta and Jogimara. Alas, I've only kept a few personal memories that are truly "human" in nature. I recall the midnight Mass in a small kitsch church of Kanchipuram, some one hundred kilometers from Chennai, where the office was celebrated in the local language. I understood nothing. But the faith of the participants was so intense that one could have, so to speak, cut it with a knife. And to appreciate this was sufficient compensation for me.[26] I recall a distressing dialogue with a colleague in New Delhi, the words of which dripped with hatred for Pakistan. And I also remember one afternoon on which, being invited to speak at a "college" in Tiruchirappalli to an audience of young girls from good families, I was going to be asked what my message was to the young Indian women. After some moments of awkward silence, I would have the inspiration to say to them: "Keep your *saris*!"

The other long stay in a foreign country was my second voyage to Brazil. I held a course in Porto Alegre in the south, a city having inhabitants essentially of Italian and German origin. I was lodged in an apartment facing a church, where the public of the daily Mass were barely different from

26. It was at Kanchipuram that I had a unique encounter, even if not quite successful, with a group of Hindus: I was conversing with the entourage of the last successor of Shankara, who had his seat in this small city. However, I strongly disappointed these philosophers who were expecting me—as was generally the case with Western thinkers who came to see them—to discover that I in fact held positions of spiritual monism. Instead, they were shown a metaphysics entirely compatible with the Christian dogmas. Result: They thought that I could no longer be received by their master.

their French and German counterparts. But, on All Saints Day, there was an office preceding the Mass. The church was filled to the point of bursting with a crowd of people of mixed origin and black, poorly dressed, and fervent. However, as soon as the office had come to an end and the Mass had commenced, the people got up and left the church . . . At Porto Alegre, I held a course on Hegel, and I "discovered" a brilliant young man. I was going to have him come to Paris, and he had in the meantime become a good specialist on Aristotle. However, apart from him, I barely had contact of any significance whatsoever. That which remains, that of which I conserve some memory, is rather a Niemeyer church, illuminated during the night in Belo Horizonte, and the sumptuous golden decorations covering the walls and the ceilings of churches in Rio and the magnificent Bahia. A third voyage to Brazil in 2009 would lead me into a changing world. This country of two hundred million inhabitants was in the process of emerging from poverty and beginning to advance in its infancy upon an uncertain route, diverting from the models of Europe and the United States.

My last significant voyage led me to Australia. In Melbourne, I was made an Honorary Professor of the Australian Catholic University. Australia is an English-speaking country with Catholic roots leading back to Ireland. The two first people among those whom I met were Father Maloney and Father Kelly! Melbourne has very agreeable neighbourhoods, and the museums of Canberra and Sydney exhibit marvelous aboriginal paintings. The nature is beautiful, the eucalyptus trees, splendid. One is able to see special farms with kangaroos, and people eat poorly—as poorly as in England and the United States. Odile had not wanted to accompany me on the twenty-two-hour flight for this voyage. And, without her, this immense country didn't leave profound traces upon me, even if I was able to enlist in the group of my "friends and disciples" an excellent Catholic student from Brisbane, a descendent of a high officer of the Sikh Light Infantry.

Australia will quite likely be the last of my important sojourns abroad. The first was in Germany, when the student of twenty-five years—three years after a linguistic trip to Frankfort—had disembarked with an Oxford scholarship and a passionate desire to study German philosophy. Freiburg im Breisgau is a city of moderate size in the south-west corner of Germany. It is a city in which the majority is Catholic, and it is at its university that Heidegger had worked for practically his entire life. This immense philosopher had just begun his retirement, and I asked his successor whether I could visit the great man. Eugen Fink responded: "If you have an important question, yes. If not, you must not forget that Martin Heidegger is not an animal in a zoo!" I did not insist . . .[27] However, this sojourn of six months didn't pass without leaving traces. I improved my German well enough to be able to read it throughout the fifty-seven years which have followed. And I was able to meet, for the last time, that profound philosopher, L. Gondos-Grünhut, who had been the inspiration for our group in Szeged, and in honor of whom I would much later publish, first in German and then in Hungarian, an anthology of his texts.[28] Odile too was in Freiburg at the beginning of this sojourn, but I was thereafter going to take classes and read philosophical works alone, little affected by the world that surrounded me. Of course, in the background of all of this persisted, in a faded, although very real manner, the awareness that this sojourn was in the country where millions of Jews were killed, and where my mother had died.

There still remains a country in which we've not spent too much time, however one to which we've felt ourselves quite attached: Canada. But more precisely, I think of its province of Quebec. We had two long stays in its capital, where I taught at Laval University. We were lodged in this old city, very close to its walls. We strolled through the streets, often quite steep, visited monuments that were not so ancient but still of very special historical significance, and my wife was enchanted to hear the Québécois accent, which made her recall the French of her native Normandy. We were able to make beautiful trips eastward. The forests in September and October with golden-brown foliage are splendid, the immense moose, more than impressive, and the lobsters, superb. We attended the daily Mass in Quebec's beautiful, classical cathedral, and a couple of years ago, we were able to participate in a healing retreat at a religious house on the edge of the Saint Lawrence. Without a doubt, the possibility of "descending" two times from Quebec to Toronto, where Nicolas, Capucine and company lived for five years, added all the more to the attractions of *la belle province*. But we also made new friends. Mr. and Mrs. de K. are a charming French-Quebec couple. And Thomas is a good philosopher. Indeed, perhaps it is necessary to remember that the figure of *le Petit Prince*, on the cover of the various editions of this marvelous little book, represents Thomas, at eight years, in

27. A Haitian pharmacy student who had housed Odile for a part of her stay in Freiburg had much more luck than I. One day, while strolling through the woods in close proximity to the city, she perceived an elderly gentleman in the act of cutting wood. A conversation had been struck when Annette, whose reading extended essentially to the magazine *Paris Match*, learnt that she had facing her Martin Heidegger in person, to whom she said: "Sir, you're a famous philosopher, but no one understands you." And Heidegger, who had never seen a black female student, began to defend himself and summarize his thinking.

28. See p. 39 n. 3.

the year that, during his short stay in Quebec, Antoine de Saint-Exupéry stayed in the house of his parents.

4.

THE VOYAGES TO AND sojourns in various countries leave their traces upon who you are, but, this being lasts, and it imposes itself as an identity. Undoubtedly, in the strict sense, one has but a single identity, one's own, that which one cannot share with anyone else, even if it has moments or faces that are equally proper to other people. I am identical, identical to myself since my birth, in fact, since my conception. But this being, or more precisely, this being-oneself, which is one reality, an ontological fact, has components, diverse identities, acquired through factors, moments of times and places, in reality according to multiple syntheses of the spatial and the temporal. Identity—one inherits and assumes it. But one assumes it only by adding to it that which is one's own. And this adding-that-which-is-one's-own is, according to all appearances, something positive and autonomous. In reality, it comes about and develops through events and encounters that nuance and sift what arises in its own right from oneself. In my case, the components of personal identity that constitute who I am, and *what* I am, comprise three specific identities, to wit, my familial identity, my Hungarian identity, and my Jewish identity. Each one of these three did I find in being born, in coming into this world. Each one of these three I have welcomed, I have accepted, I have wedded and developed. My familial identity, as that of a married person having children and grandchildren, exists and has continued from an extraordinary synthesis of that which is given and that which is chosen and willed. The familial identity is most powerfully determined by that which is unconscious, by factors of blood. But it exists and also continues through the freest movements of a human being, having one go out from oneself in order to marry oneself to another. And the familial identity of each man is splintered by community identities. These issue above all from the basis of national and religious affiliations, from belonging to a people and belonging to a church. But, in my case, all of that is complicated: I am Hungarian, but I no longer live in Hungary; I'm Jewish, but I've become Christian.

The familial identity is composed of what one is and what one becomes, that is to say, of one's family of birth, of the one one has joined, and, above all, of the one one has called into existence. My family of birth is in Hungary. Over these sixty plus years in the West, I have continued to maintain affectionate contact with those who stayed in Hungary, and with those who left for Israel. Since the death of Aunt Kató in 2016, the first cousin of my mother, I've been the eldest of this family, which in the end is gathered only through memories and sentiments, of this family in which, with the exception of my brother, his children, and his grandchildren, no one is a believer, of this family dispersed into the world. As for those who make up what the French so prettily call the "*belle-famille*,"[29] there is indeed proximity and affection. But what "identity" could one discern between the grandson of a Jewish landowner in the west of Hungary and the descendants of a Norman notary? There remains, therefore, according to its plentitude, only the elementary identity that one feels with those who arise from one's marriage: one's children, and grandchildren.

For me, this elementary identity, the most intense born from bloodlines, would be "developed" during the long years of familial life in the United States and in France. It is necessary, therefore, to ask: What are *my* links to these two countries, to these two worlds? Things are simpler for that which concerns America. We lived there for twelve years. Each time we return there, we feel, in a certain manner, at home. But America is not my country. I have an immense respect for the Great Nation; I am appreciative toward it. Appreciative, notably for its having contributed, in a decisive manner, to rescuing the world from the Nazis, for having saved the world from Soviet Communism, for representing the ultimate aid in the face of possible future attacks against Western countries, and not only against the West. I have expressed, without realizing it very well, this appreciation through the large book devoted to the greatest thinker of Puritan America, Jonathan Edwards.[30] Has this book been able to settle my debts to the country of Roosevelt and Reagan? I don't know. All I know is that my sentiments toward America are those of a man who—while admiring the America where he spent many years of his life and carried out the most interesting part of his career—in no manner belongs there. What, therefore, of my links to France, the country in which I passed more than half of my life? Here, things are of course quite different. It is France which had welcomed the young political refugee. It is France which had adopted him for his studies and philosophical work. It is France which had permitted him to deepen his Catholic faith. It is the place where he met his spouse. It is in France that I've now lived for over forty years, and it's in French that I've written my books. However, can I call France *my* country?

29. [Trans.] The French "*belle-famille*" literally translates to "beautiful family" or "sweetheart's family," which in English one contently refers to as one's "in-laws."

30. *La Pensée de Jonathan Edwards*. The English translation of this emblematic book [*The Thought of Jonathan Edwards*] has gone to press (see the bibliography), and its Hungarian translation is in preparation.

It did not escape Odile's notice that when I announced a trip to Budapest in 1989 (the year that the Communist Regime in Hungary collapsed), I said for the first time: "I'm going to *my home*." I love France, and I defend her in the face of criticism and attack. I also say, while talking of the Paris apartment in which I live: "This is *our* apartment." Or again: "We are returning to *our home* from a trip." But, even if I'm a French citizen, impassioned by the political life of the Fifth Republic, France has never been, nor ever will it be, my country. My country, my homeland, was and remains Hungary.

I was born in Hungary, and until my twentieth year, I wasn't able to leave this country. It was obvious that I was Hungarian, a fact upon which I'd never reflected, an obviousness that I'd never put into question. I was born into a family of intense patriotic tradition. My great great grandfather was an officer of the Hungarian Revolution of 1848. My grandfather was vice-president of the governmental party of his county. As for my adoptive father, having arrived at the John F. Kennedy International Airport in 1965, the first words that he addressed to me after eight years of separation were: "Don't forget that you're Hungarian!" To be sure, I've not forgotten the fact that I was born and raised Hungarian, that I come from a strongly patriotic family. However, during the 1960s, the very idea of one day being able to return to the country of my birth began to lose all probability, all pertinence. But with certain international political developments in the Sixties, and above all based on my access to French nationality, this return had become possible. The day after I obtained certification of my French nationality, I went to the Hungarian Consulate in Paris in order to obtain a visa. And we (Odile, myself, and the two small boys) effectively left for Budapest. A few minutes before our arrival at the border between Austria and Hungary, I became so distressed that I had to ask my wife to take the wheel. But a short while later, I took it back from her. In fact, it was easier to *do* something than to passively await the sight of the barbed wire and watchtowers that separated the People's Republic from the Imperialist West! In Budapest, I was reunited with family and friends, and over the years that have followed, I—we—continued to visit the country of my birth, which my wife also very much loves and appreciates, and the language of which she has even undertaken to learn. These were but "private" visits. However, in 1984, I was able to organize for myself to present lectures at the universities of Budapest and Szeged. I'd never written philosophy in my mother tongue, so I drafted my text in French, and then, with the aid of a dictionary, translated all of it into Hungarian. But my hosts requested that I speak on subjects other than those which I had myself chosen. I obliged, but I was then struck by something overwhelming: While writing my lectures, I realized that I in fact possessed my maternal language. And this put me in a strange state, whereby I forgot for a short while my life and my family in France in order to find myself Hungarian in Hungary. From that moment, in an irregular but uninterrupted manner, I held classes mainly in Budapest, and from time to time also in Szeged. And from 2009 until 2014, thus for five years, I was going to organize numerous Franco-Hungarian philosophy conferences at the French Institute of Budapest. I have been able to recommence something analogous in 2018, just as I again began to hold courses in the spring of 2017 at the University of Szeged.

Until then, all seemed very simple. The Hungarian who had made his life in a foreign land, and who had never forgotten his roots, had reestablished contact, as soon as it was possible, with his country of birth, where he began to organize professional events, and also see the publication of some of his books in his mother tongue. But things are not as simple as they appear. This Hungarian octogenarian who received important Hungarian titles and medals, who has important friends in contemporary Hungary, is a Hungarian of Jewish origin, and Hungary is a country of strong antisemitic tradition. One still sees signs on the walls of Budapest: "Jews into the Danube!" To be sure, these signs are quickly effaced, but they reappear just as quickly . . . And if one listened to the people in the metro or in their homes, one would frequently hear miserable and odious statements. Without a doubt, memory of the horrors of 1944 and '45 prevented one from expressing one's antisemitism in public, but the phrase of one of the great actors of the Forties remains, alas, pertinent. One day, he was asked to provide a definition of antisemitism, and this is the wisecrack he presented as a reply: "An anti-Semite is one who detests Jews more than necessary."

With this bending of the Hungarian identity in the direction of antisemitism, I pick up the third of my main identities: the Jewish identity. I was born Jewish, by Jewish parents, who did not however want to have me circumcised. No one in my family apart from my paternal grandmother was a practicing Jew, but even she had the Sabbath bean dish served with ham in it. Of the members of my maternal family, my mother's sister, her husband, and her son were Zionists, but "secular" Zionists who had nothing to do with the Jewish faith, with the Law, or prayer. For the emancipated Jews of the countries of Central Europe, including Hungary, to be Jewish was a qualification of survival: survival of practices and precepts, of thoughts and beliefs—but practices which were no longer practiced, and beliefs in which one no longer believed. The qualification "emancipated Jew" had a significance and implications as much positive as negative. Those negative were the uncertainty and malaise of everyday life. The Jews would have desperately loved not to be known or noticed as Jews. Most of them did all they could to avoid appearing Jewish. Of course, in the family and among friends, these men and women revealed and attested to their Jewish-being, but once the circle of family or friends became publicly noticeable, one found oneself hesitant and awkward. Must one admit that one is Jewish, or should one try to conceal this point of fact? And if one opted for silence, secrecy, even dissimulation, could one hope that these efforts were going to bear success? Could one believe that those whom one recognizes in the street or in the office, in businesses, or in libraries, could themselves ignore that one was Jewish? Do there exist sure ways to be hidden by a hat, to be covered by a cloak, to be disguised? Most of us were trying our luck, but we were equally skeptical about our chances of success. We used to wonder, therefore, with feelings of faintness and fear, whether we had been found out, and from our side, we never ceased scrutinizing those whom we would meet: Were they not themselves perhaps also Jews? The truth is that there were numerous "Christians" who were in fact Jews. And in our hearts, we were ready to suppose, before the contrary could be proven, that many of those whom we met and crossed were well and truly children of Abraham, Israelites.

However, if there were many Jews who would have wanted to hide their true identity at any cost, they nonetheless felt respect and admiration for this qualification, which, for various reasons, they would have wanted to dissimulate. Despite opinions and prejudices of most of their non-Jewish compatriots, the Jews are thought of and known as honest and upright in business. They're also thought of and known as generous and charitable. And, above all, they are known as more intelligent and more gifted than their compatriot "goys." During almost two thousand years of confinement to communities wherein life revolved around the knowledge and observance of practices, the Jews came to have an unbounded respect for things of the mind. Hence, they developed a cast of scholars and thinkers, whom they cherished and extolled. And when the ghettos began to open, the dispersal of the Jews into social life constituted a veritable explosion. The intellectual professions were invaded by Jews, notably medicine and law. The renowned research institutions—universities and laboratories—of Europe and America were overflowing with the descendants of those people of letters who emerged from the ghettos. This was the way in which things happened in Germany, in Austria, and perhaps still more strongly in Hungary, the country which poured out dozens, hundreds of mathematicians, physicists, sociologists, and philosophers into countries more developed in research institutions and less strictly discriminatory against this galaxy of learned descendants of Abraham and Moses.

Undoubtedly, the great majority of Jews of Central Europe, of Hungary, did not possess these extraordinary talents. But they believed no less in belonging to a superior kind. To be Jewish meant to be peaceful and proper, a lover of things of the mind, intelligent and knowledgeable. The student that I was, the young boy, then an adolescent, had been raised in this tradition. He was considered to be a gifted Jew, disposed to knowledge, and destined for intellectual activity, an intellectual profession. But this excellence had barely any veritable religious components. Quite to the contrary, I completely ignored all that which came from the Jewish religion, and I had no inclination to take notice of it. Before my conversion in 1954, the Jewish religion, like all other religion, seemed to me to be nonsense, a kind of non-being. I needed to make no effort to keep it out of my sight, nor any effort to turn my attention toward it. But things could not fail to change once I had become a Christian. I was going to believe in Catholic dogma, rooted in the teaching of the Bible, and even if the New Testament henceforth had stronger significance for my faith, it was quite necessary to admit that the Old Testament was its origin, its base, and therefore continued to have great worth. The "solution" at which I arrived was the same as that of other Jews who had converted to Christianity: The Old Testament certainly belongs to our theological baggage, constituting part of the data of our faith; but this Old Testament, which prepared for the New Testament, was also subsumed by it. I was Jewish, and this was something very precious, but my roots, my Jewish origins, were integrated into my Christian present, and Christianity is simply the realization, the accomplishment, of all that is true in the Israelite religion.

But an event had intervened now fifteen years ago. In an odious article, a communist historian explained that during the Second World War, the Catholic hierarchy in Eastern Europe participated in the pillaging of Jewish property. I wrote a response to these lies, which *Le Monde* would publish. And after, I addressed myself to Father Lustiger in order to have him recommend me to a place, a movement, which would help me better comprehend the relations between Israel and the Church, and, consequently, my own condition of being a Jewish Christian. He indicated to me a group composed of both Jews who had become Christians and their spouses, as well as others among the Catholic religious, engaged in various movements for the purpose of attaining a better understanding of the theological lines between Israel and the Church. The fifteen years of belonging to this group have led me to realize that one could, and should, go further than denouncing antisemitism and holding meetings with one's "brother" Jews. Rather, one could, and even should, reflect upon the mysterious continuation of the presence of the Lord in Israel, even after the Incarnation of the Son. I carried out some reading, and I ended up developing relationships with Messianic friends who intend to recognize and profess the totality of Christian dogma, all while searching for ways to reconcile this faith with the continuing existence of a Jewish people. However, in that which concerns me personally, the problematic has no veritable existential significance. On an intellectual, conceptual plane, my condition as a Jewish Christian can be the object of an interrogation, but it barely has significance concerning my identities. I am Jewish because I descend from Jewish parents and ancestors, which means that I am of Jewish blood. I am Jewish because I share Jewish attitudes and values, but attitudes and values proper to *secularized* Jews. And I am Catholic because I confess the Catholic faith, because I belong to the Catholic Church.

5.

All of these identities are gathered and united in the Catholic identity, the force, the power, which accomplishes and articulates their synthesis. I discovered God, I discovered the Catholic faith, with neither cause nor reason, and this gracious discovery continues to furnish and nourish a pure faith, pure not from the moral point of view, but quite simply in that it is not mixed with anything else that could explain its coming to be and continuation. I received the Faith suddenly, without any preparation, in a single instant, unnuanced, without interior or exterior relation. And I essentially continue to "have" it in this foundational manner. The discovery-without-reason of my faith determined its incessant practice, also utterly pure, also stripped of reason, but which in the capacity of practice, in the capacity of action, in the capacity of comportment, must take forms, wed itself to content. These forms and this content depend on the one and only principle of the Faith. They expose it and articulate it in certain manners that one can feel and experience as imperfect, as precarious, as inadequate, even not truly faithful. But all of this lack, all of these discontinuities are not what is essential. What is essential is that they attest, in their fragmentary, imperfect manner, to the movement toward a term, a term which is as much already attained as it is remaining to be attained.

Faith is therefore the principle of a life. But it is equally a teaching: a teaching on the essential, on our relation to God, on God. But man also has at his disposal another possibility to discover the foundations, the profound truths, the essential, and this possibility is given in and through philosophy. I began to do philosophy in Szeged, and I continued this work by opting, on my arrival in France, for studies in philosophy at the Sorbonne. And this choice is not unrelated to my religious preoccupations. It is not so much about the "demonstration" of the truth of my beliefs. Rather, it has as its purpose the explanation of things to which beliefs are directed in a manner other than that of faith. I have never stopped aiming for the Principle, but I wanted to take as many detours as necessary, that is, as many preparations as required, for me to approach this, or rather Him in Whom I believe. I am a philosopher. I have written much. Including second editions (even a third edition for my book on Simone Weil) and translations into foreign languages, some fifty books bear my name. My activity as a philosophical writer has followed three different paths. I began by presenting conceptual analyses of mysticism and spirituality,[31] and even one of my very last books, the one on Fénelon, enters into that category. But if this preoccupation, this interest persists, it now finds itself in the shadow of my works on the history of philosophy, more particularly, those which treat German idealism. My most important book deals with the two *paths* that have followed Kant and his successors.[32] The first way is that of a conceptual speculation, notably in Hegel, which is related to the whole real, but which finds its completion, its recapitulation, in a reformulation of the major themes and theses of Christianity. The second is the one that above all represents Kant himself, which separates the appearances and the things-in-themselves. We know our world, teaches critical philosophy, but on the plane of appearances. However, *there*, one is in a position to obtain a rigorous and coherent knowledge. As for the foundations of the real, these are the things-in-themselves to which the appearances relate: One certainly cannot truly know them, but one knows that they have worth, and that they are. Suffice it to say that in the face of a coherent and systematic knowledge of the world, albeit limited to the plane of appearances, one preserves the clear certitude of the existence of supreme realities.

My studies on Christian mystiques and German idealists carry on in very different worlds, but each one of these worlds is a work, and my studies are works on the works of thinkers other than myself. However, for the last ten or so years, I have felt myself capable of developing *my own* thought. First, this was through *The Expansion of Metaphysics* (2012),[33] a systematic exposé of the essential structures of our world. Subsequently came the *Court traité sur l'amour*,[34] which presents the marvelous realities of human love, but with a reflection upon divine love as its point of departure. And I have just started writing *God: A Philosophical Study*. Once this work has been finished, I think—or, let us say, conjecture—that I will be close enough

31. *La Métaphysique religieuse de Simone Weil.* [English translation: *The Religious Metaphysics of Simone Weil.*]

32. *De Kant à Schelling*, 2 vols. (A German translation was published in 2018.)

33. [Trans.] 2018 for the English translation.

34. L'Harmattan, 2020.

to be able to directly check whether what I will have written actually corresponds to the truth! And with this preoccupation, I arrive at the essential, at the ultimate, at the Faith.

My philosophical works have their independence *sui generis*. They have worth in and for themselves. The fact that they have permitted me to practice a profession that makes me live can also refer to their metaphysical status as *sui generis* worldly realities. However, my philosophical thoughts also constitute a kind of twin counterpart to my beliefs. They are certainly not claimed to prove or judge these beliefs, but they help to "better" understand them, to present approaches to them, appreciations of them. Many philosophical reflections of mine are inspired by the truths of faith, and, in their turn, these reflections render possible a presentation of such truths other than the one offered by theology. Must I recall each one? I could, certainly, enumerate a series of religious truths, present the list of the dogmas that I profess. However, certain among them are, so to speak, fundamental, and recognition of them can serve to better comprehend as well as more clearly and more fervently appreciate all of the others. Christianity teaches that God is triune, that is to say, He is personal, and philosophy shows and demonstrates that one is not a person but with another person. The foundational core and motor of personal-being is to love, and love is something free and gratuitous. However, if there were only two, this would be a sterile reciprocity, in which affection would be exhausted in a *do ut des*, an exchange in which one gives and one receives, but with one giving only as much as one receives, and one receiving only as much as one gives. Marriage illustrates this truth in the human sphere: The love between man and wife does not find its accomplishment but in its going-toward and living-within other beings—children. As for divine love, it is trinitary. The Trinity, through and beyond the numerical form, expresses the freedom and inexhaustible gratuity of this love among persons. And this gratuity equally permits the work of the Divinity toward those other than Itself. This work manifests itself first in Creation, the call from out of nothingness, and then in the Incarnation, in order to deliver, to save this created world fallen into sin.

The dogmas are the principles and the structures of my faith, which I received like a stone—or rather like a bomb—fallen from on high. It came from elsewhere to throw itself into an emptiness, a void. It filled this void, but, strangely, the void remains. Without a doubt, I have had some sudden and strong "religious experiences," however, the light which emanated from them was, so to speak, instantaneous. The darkness returns, or rather, it remains. I practice my faith, I attend Mass practically every day, I begin my day with an office, meditations, prayer, but the void persists. In returning to Communion, I "awake" all of a sudden to recognize that I just received the Body of Christ upon my lips. Reading the texts of the office for the day, I realize suddenly that I have read them until the end, but that I no longer remember what I read. Religion fills me, dominates me. It has caused me to live and to act, but the void continues within and around me. This void corresponds, so to speak, with the coming of Christ, Who, while having taken flesh, remains in the heart of the Father. The Son is the Lamb Who has come to take away the sin of the world. Yes, the ecclesial teaching on original sin is absolutely essential for me. A foundational dogma, although very often resisted by sad people who digest poorly. I, from time to time, get angry, but I'm mostly joyous. As for digestion, there's no problem, notably for heavy Hungarian cured meats and substantial chocolate cakes. Suffice it to say that I approve of joy, happiness, and the pleasures of this life, as well as the joy, happiness, and pleasures of faith, bestowed by grace, the conqueror of evil. But this is the conqueror in a victory which, while being radical, cannot make me forget the abysses which surround me and which persist within me. I live, therefore, in joy with Jesus Christ, but how do I, or how should I, live therein?

The Christian faith has two essential commandments: love God and love thy neighbor. These two commandments are inseparable, but the love of God is the first.[35] We live this faith which professes two loves in the Church, a church founded by Christ, the holy, catholic, apostolic, and Roman church, a church infallible in its teachings, and which is a place of life, a church which is a community, our belonging to which determines, accompanies, and delineates the moments and the steps of all our existence. We share this belonging with an innumerable multitude of other men and women, and it facilitates the encounters, the contacts, the friendships with these others. This belonging, founded upon faith, is at the origin of the life that we live. I am Catholic, which signifies that I must—let us say, rather, that I should—live according to the intuitions and the commandments of this faith which guides me. To be sure, I do not interrogate myself at each instant about whether that which I do, or that which I do not, conforms or does not conform to the ecclesial teachings. Such an interrogation is not necessary. The profound principles of Christian morality have penetrated our society, at least on a theoretical, normative plane. We are supposed to affirm and practice the good, even if we know very well that the affirmation and the practice of this good are only very, very imperfectly possible for us. We know how we should feel and act, and the principles and institutions which govern our society make us recognize, without too much difficulty,

35. Matthew 22:34[–40]. Among other things, that means: The Lamb of God has come first to take away the sin of the world, and only very secondarily to found Christian syndicates.

almost immediately, when we fail in our duties. But there is a domain in which all unity and all correspondence disappears. Our society has divorced itself from the Christian teaching on marriage. According to the doctrine that the Catholic Church professes, marriage is a union between a man and a woman, and it extends toward the gift of the child. It is one, indissoluble here below, and we hope that it will be continued, even if we in no manner know how. But this is no longer clear for the world that surrounds us. It in no way conceives the indissolubility of the relationship, nor the obvious implication of the openness of the conjugal union to the child. As for us, Odile and I, we feel as though we're on a small, happy island in the fifty-sixth year of our marriage. Our eldest son is a priest, and our second son and our daughter live in fervent faith and happy marriages with numerous children. What more is there to say?

At eighty-two years of age, we are tempted to make a kind of evaluation, while waiting for others to do it for us. I've had a happy existence, full of grace, but an existence led in the midst of perils, dramas, and tragedies. I've experienced and suffered them, but in such a way that they did not prevent me from advancing. I've been able to advance, and also have others advance. I knew that I was gifted, very gifted, but I've also met, occasionally, those more gifted than me. I've worked a lot. I've made sacrifices. In brief, I've paid prices, and alas, I've also made those around me pay prices. I believe to have succeeded, even if I would have loved to succeed even more, and that goes for everything: for faith, for family, for the production of books. So, the question arises: What would I do if I could start all over again? To be sure, this is an ultimately absurd question, for one is unique in space and time. How, therefore, could one start again? If, however, one could do it, quite probably, I'd do the same things that in this life I've actually done. Why? Because they were in their manner "good," and also because I think that I wouldn't have been able to do otherwise. It therefore only remains for me to express my gratitude for all of this: what I've had and who I've been, what I have and who I am. I thank those who are closest to me, but also those who are or were further from me. And I thank Him, Who called me into life, and to life with Him.

Marriage with Odile Wattré in the church of Neufchâtel-en Bray (July 3, 1962)

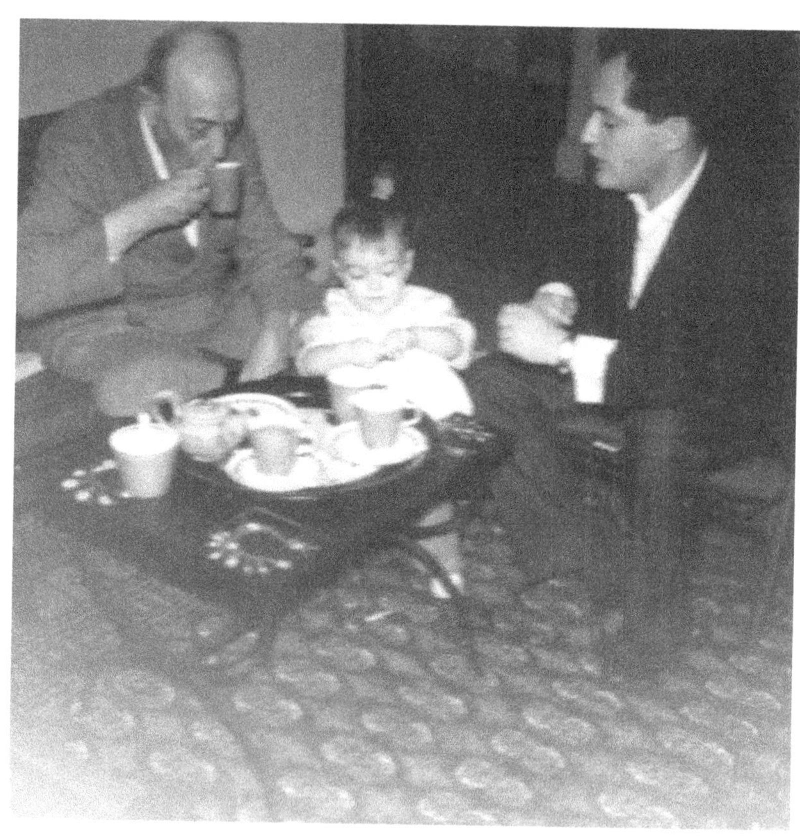

With Miklós Vető (1895–1968), adoptive father, Hamden, Connecticut, United States, and our eldest son, Étienne (December 1965)

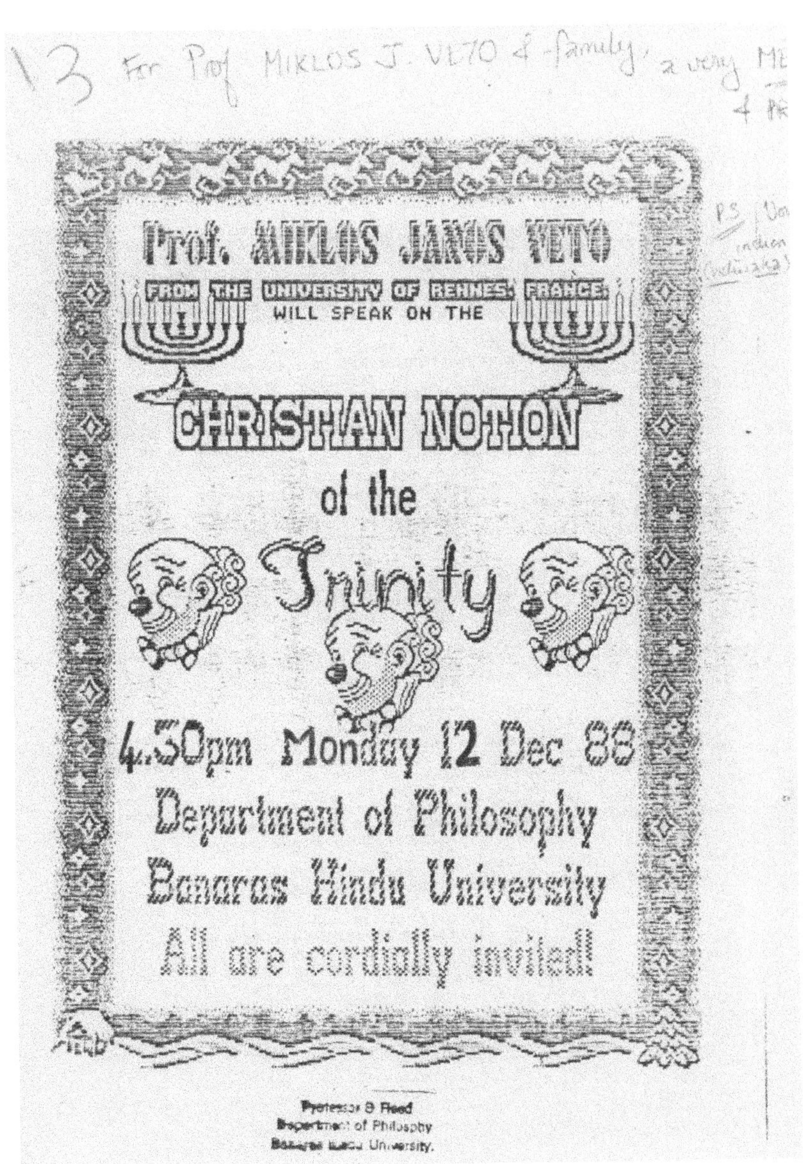

Lecture at the Banaras Hindu University (December 12, 1988)

With John Paul II, Rome (January 5, 1990)

Paris identity photo (1993?)

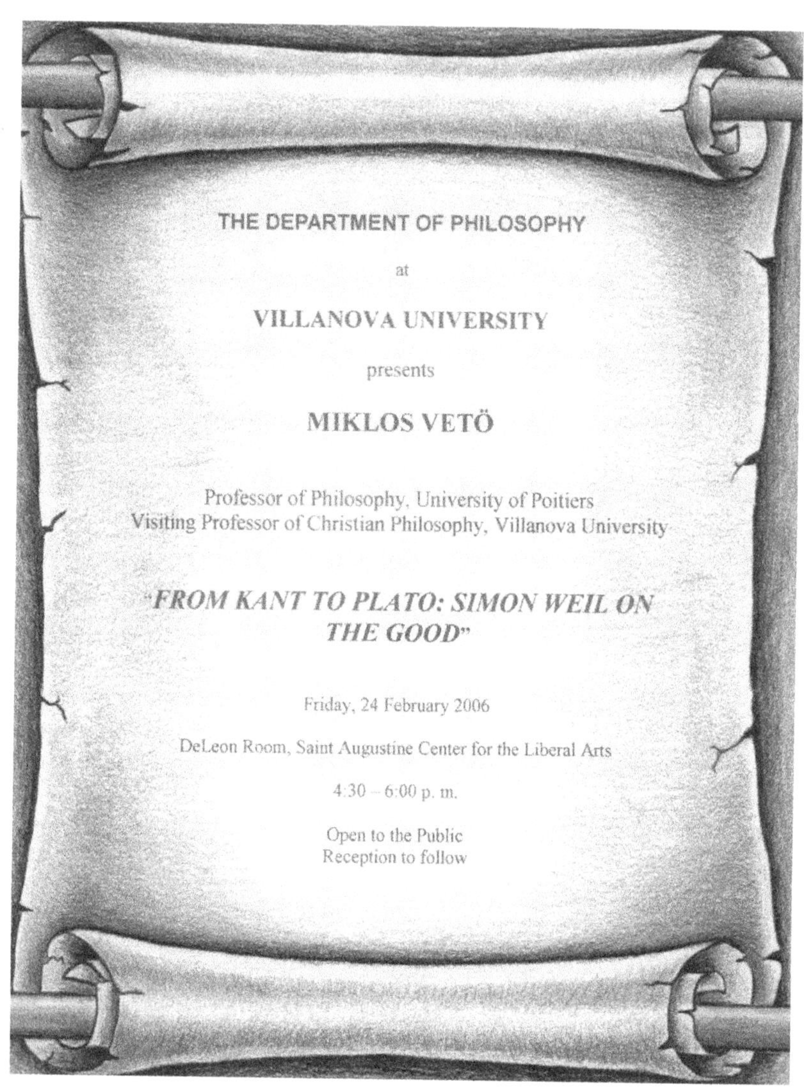

Lecture at Villanova University (2006)

Celebration of the election as External Member
of the Hungarian Academy of Sciences, Budapest (June 2008)

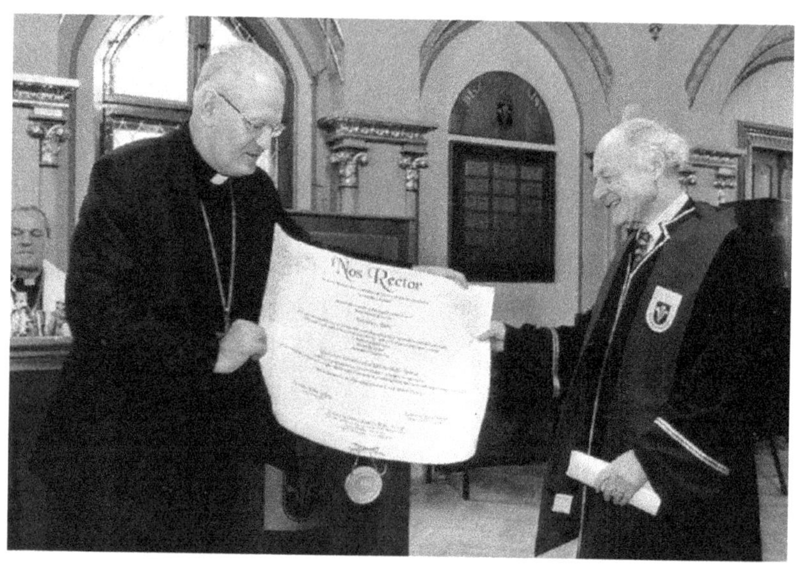

Reception of the diploma of *Doctor Honoris Causa*,
Pázmány Péter Catholic University, Budapest, from the hand of Cardinal Péter Erdö,
Primate of the Catholic Church of Hungary (December 10, 2010)

Lecture during the presentation of the diploma

Meeting at The University of Abidjan (June, 2014)

In Ivorian formal dress, Paris

Chronology

1936	August 22: Birth in Budapest, to parents Vető János Zsigmond (1901–1941) and Aczél Eva (1907–1945)
1938	July 4: Birth of my brother, István
1941	May 14: Death of my father May 17: Baptism June: Expulsion of the family from Felcsút, departure for Budapest
1943	September–April 1944: Primary school in Budapest December 23: Death of my grandmother, Ilona Vető
1944	March 19: The Germans occupy Hungary May: My mother takes me to the home of my adoptive parents July: My mother is deported to Germany October 17–December 10: Accommodated in a convent November: Deportation of my adoptive father to Germany December 10: I am brought with István to the home of my adoptive mother December 24–January 31, 1945: We live in a cellar
1945	End of March: Trip from Budapest to Mohács with my adoptive mother April 4: Liberation of Hungary by the Red Army End of May: I reunite with István in the Felcsút house, temporally regained by the family Mid-August: Return of my adoptive father from deportation 1945–1946: Szemere utca Primary School in Budapest
1946	September: Admission to the French section of Madách High School (first admitted in the entry examination)

1947	First publication: a small text on the art of East Asia in the high school journal August: István leaves Felcsút and comes to live with Aunt Irén in Budapest
1948	The year of the Turn (the coming of communist dictatorship) in Hungary December 31: Nationalization of our mine, the only source of revenue for many members of our family
1949	The teaching of Western languages is practically suppressed, Russian replacing them
1952	Discovery of Baudelaire
1953	Commencement of the reading of Thomas Mann, Dostoyevsky, and Tolstoy
1954	Third Friday of the month of February: Foundational religious experience June: I win the second prize in the National Studies Competition in history June: High school diploma At the start of September: Departure for Szeged, where I undertake legal studies November–December: I make the acquaintance of Ferenc Kiefer and János Aszalós
1955	July: Military service in Tapolca
1956	October 16: Foundation of the MEFESZ in Szeged October 23: Hungarian Revolution November 4: Entry of the Red Army into Hungary; constitution of the J. Kádár Government
1957	February 6: Escape to Yugoslavia February–May: Successive stays in various refugee camps in Yugoslavia May 17: Arrival in France, in the refugee camp of Montbéliard May 27: I arrive in Paris November: Commencement of studies in philosophy at the Sorbonne; I begin to frequent the Richelieu Center
1959	November: Commencement of life in Oxford
1960	May: I meet Odile in front of the Sorbonne Autumn: Iris Murdoch accepts me for a thesis on Simone Weil
1961	July–December: Study sojourn in Freiburg im Breisgau
1962	July 2: Civil marriage July 3: Religious marriage September: Commencement of our life in Oxford

1963	June: Defense and failure of my thesis August: Our arrival in New York, then in Milwaukee; we become lecturers at Marquette University
1964	Oxford accepts my slightly revised thesis Autumn: I am recruited to Yale for the following academic period (1965–1974) November 28: Birth of Étienne December 13: Death of my mother in Budapest
1965	September: Arrival in New Haven, and moving into our house; my father reunites with us for approximately three months
1966	Odile is nominated to Yale
1967	November 19: Birth of Nicolas
1968	March 7: Death of my father in Budapest
1970	March: I am naturalized as a French citizen April: First familial trip to Budapest Autumn: I commence participating in the meetings of the Charismatic Renewal (Hamden and New Haven)
1971	Publication of my first book *La Métaphysique religieuse de Simone Weil* [*The Religious Metaphysics of Simone Weil*] September 9: Birth of Marie-Élisabeth
1974	May: I defend, in Paris, my *thèse d'État* (D. Litt) on Schelling
1975–1979	Professor at The University of Abidjan, Ivory Coast (as French collaborator)
1977	*Le Fondement selon Schelling* [*The Ground According to Schelling*]
1979	Return to France and nomination to the University of Rennes I
1981	Commencement of meetings of our prayer group in Rennes
1987	*La Pensée de Jonathan Edwards* [*The Thought of Jonathan Edwards*]
1989	Hungary once again finds its independence
1991	Odile retires from teaching October: Marriage of Capucine and Nicolas
1992	January–May: *Fellow, Center of Theological Inquiry*, Princeton September: Transfer to the University of Poitiers December: Birth of the first of our grandchildren
1993	June: Relocating to Paris
1994	September: Marriage of Marie-Élisabeth and Didier
1997	September: Ordination of Étienne
1998–2000	*De Kant à Schelling* [*From Kant to Schelling*], volumes 1 and 2

2002	*La Naissance de la Volonté* [*The Birth of the Will*]
2005	I retire from the University of Poitiers
2006	January–May: Professor of Christian Philosophy, Villanova University
2007, 2010	Visiting Professor to the Laval University, Quebec
2008	May: External Member of the Hungarian Academy of Sciences
2010	December: Reception of *Doctorate Honoris Causa*, Pázmány Péter Catholic University, Budapest and Piliscsaba
2012	*L'Élargissement de la Métaphysique* [*The Expansion of Metaphysics*]
2015	October–November: Honorary Professor, Australian Catholic University, Melbourne
2016	November: Reception of *Doctorate Honoris Causa*, University of Szeged
2017	Commencement of the writing of *Dieu. Étude philosophique* [*God. A Philosophical Study*]
2020	*January 8: death in Paris* *Posthumous publication of* Court Traité sur l'Amour [Short Treatise on Love]

Appendix: Related Documents

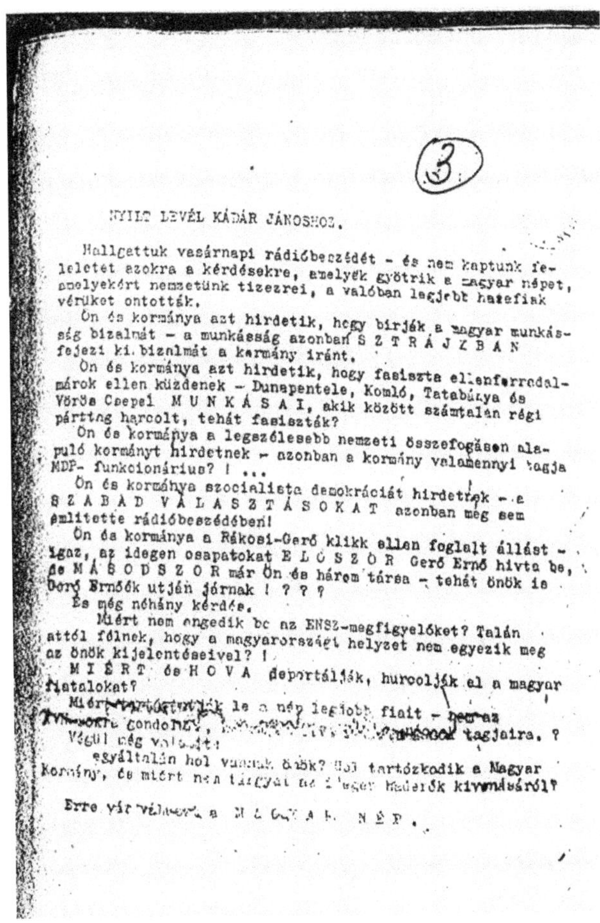

3

NYILT LEVÉL KÁDÁR JÁNOSHOZ.

Hallgattuk vasárnapi rádióbeszédét – és nem kaptunk feleletet azokra a kérdésekre, amelyek gyötrik a magyar népet, amelyekért nemzetünk tizezrei, a valóban legjobb hazafiak vérüket ontották.

Ön és kormánya azt hirdetik, hogy birják a magyar munkásság bizalmát – a munkásság azonban S Z T R Á J K B A N fejezi ki bizalmát a kormány iránt.

Ön és kormánya azt hirdetik, hogy fasiszta ellenforradalmárok ellen küzdenek – Dunapentele, Komló, Tatabánya és Vörös Csepel M U N K Á S A I, akik között számtalan régi párttag harcolt, tehát fasiszták?

Ön és kormánya a legszélesebb nemzeti összefogáson alapuló kormányt hirdetnek – azonban a kormány valamennyi tagja MDP- funkcionárius? ! ...

Ön és kormánya szocialista demokráciát hirdetnek – a S Z A B A D V Á L A S Z T Á S O K A T azonban még sem említette rádióbeszédében!

Ön és kormánya a Rákosi-Gerő klikk ellen foglalt állást – igaz, az idegen csapatokat E L Ő S Z Ö R Gerő Ernő hivta be, de M Á S O D S Z O R már Ön és három társa – tehát önök is Gerő Ernőék utján járnak ! ? ? ?

És még néhány kérdés.

Miért nem engedik be az ENSZ-megfigyelőket? Talán attól félnek, hogy a magyarországi helyzet nem egyezik meg az önök kijelentéseivel? !

M I É R T és H O V A deportálják, hurcolják el a magyar fiatalokat?

Miért [illegible] le a nép legjobb fiait – [illegible] condoln[illegible] tagjaira. ?

Végül még [illegible]:

egyáltalán hol vannak önök? Hol tartózkodik a Magyar Kormány, és miért nem [illegible] Kádárék kivonásáról?

Erre vár választ a M A G Y A R N É P.

Open letter to János Kádár, head of the government, mid-November, 1956

Translation[1]

OPEN LETTER TO JÁNOS KÁDÁR[2]

We have heard your speech delivered by radio on Sunday—yet we have not received any response to the questions which torment the Hungarian people, for which tens of thousands of our nation, the best patriots, shed their blood.

You and your government announce fighting against a fascist counter-revolution—the WORKERS of Dunapentele, of Komló, of Tatabánya, of the Red Csepel,[3] in the middle of which a very great number of the Party combatted, are therefore fascists?

You and your government announce a government based on the broadest national consensus, however all of the members of the government are officials of the Communist Party.

You and your government announce a socialist democracy, but you did not even mention FREE ELECTIONS in your radio speech.

You and your government have taken a position against the Rákosi-Gerő clique.[4] Certainly, it was Ernő Gerő who called foreign troops for the FIRST TIME, but for the SECOND TIME it was you and your three companions. Thus, you march on the same path as Gerő.

And still some questions:

Why did you not let the observers from the United Nations enter? Perhaps you fear that the current situation in Hungary does not correspond to your declarations?

WHY and WHERE do you haul around, where you deport the young Hungarians?

Why do you jail the best children of the people? We think not of the members of the Secret Police, but of the [illegible text].

And finally:

1. The translations of these documents have been made by our care, except for the one in Arabic, which has been translated by Mr. M. Fattal. [Translations into English are from the French, with exception to the documents already presented in English, in which cases their French translations are omitted.]

2. The Soviets, after having crushed the Revolution, had installed János Kádár as head of the Hungarian Government.

3. Worker locations *par excellence* of the country.

4. Mátyás Rákosi, communist dictator of Hungary between 1948 and 1956, and Ernő Gerő, his successor, overthrown by the Revolution.

Where are you in fact located? Where does the Hungarian Government reside, and why does it not discuss the subject of the withdrawal of foreign troops?

It is to these questions that the HUNGARIAN PEOPLE await a response.

Cedar Lodge
Steeple Aston
Oxford

Dear Nicholas,
I return these with commentary. I have to go to London & doubt if I can see you before you go.
I have made little alterations of English in the text itself, & the other (mostly minor) comments in the two enclosed sheets.
I think this stuff is good, indeed very good. Your

method of exposition has improved greatly, & your English is far better: you now have a style, which is a notable feat! I admire the way in which you've brought out the very difficult ideas & arranged to fit them so convincingly together.
I feel great confidence in your hero. I think the Introduction is absolutely right in tone — it has the right impersonal air of authority. And note 8, yes, certainly in place!

(That neat aside might please your examiners!) The introduction, while being impersonal, puts you on the map and makes suitably clear the nature of your interest in SW. You'd better just change the reference to linguistic philosophy (see my suggestion) on page 4! After all, they come in all kinds now.
Apropos my rebuke in my note on page 1 of Time and the Ego, I have just looked in the Oxford dictionary & find that the word "constate" does exist! "Rare, 1773".

So I think you'd better not use it! Anyway, your punishment is cancelled!
Altogether I think your stuff is really interesting & sound — it's certainly taught me a lot!
What a marvellous mind she has & how many true things she knows!
Apropos your Introduction page 5, is it so unusual for theologians to think of the Trinity, Incarnation, etc as somehow "written into the structure of the universe"! She is so convincing on this, she practically converts me!

Best affection [illegible] Christmas [illegible] (I.M.)

Letter from Iris Murdoch, December 1962[5]

5. [This note combines two notes in the original French edition.] [The mention of *Time and the Ego*] concerns the work of Heidegger, *Being and Time*. Iris Murdoch (1919–1999) was a British philosopher and novelist.

Dossziészám: 02 F-D 0110-875-2 VHE

V-145252

TERHELŐ ADATOK FELSOROLÁSA: I.

1956. októberi események során a szegedi egyetemen ellenforradalmi röplapok készitésében és terjesztésében vett részt.

Nyugatra disszidált 1956-ban. Magával vitt egy államtitkot képező, ÁVH. tanulmányi anyagot.

27

Lakcíme ismeretlen

Családi és utóneve: VETŐ MIKLÓS 04
(Asszonyok leányneve):

Előző neve:

Asszonyok férjezett neve:

Születési helye: Budapest

év, hó, nap: 1936.

Anyja neve: ACZÉL ÉVA

Foglalkozása: 1945 előtt: jelenleg: joghallgató

Iskolai végzettsége: gimn. érettségi

Párttagsága:

Lakhely: megye: Budapest, XIII.ker. város, község: Sallai u.8.

Munkahelye:

Állampolgársága: magyar

Budapest, 1964. év jun. hó 11. n.

Osztály—alosztály: III/2/C.

Tóth Béláné r.fhdgy aláírás

Ellenőrizte: [illegible] alosztályvezető

008940

Dossziészám:

II.

Dossziészám:

IV.

Dossziészám:

III.

1965 MAR 22
1966 JAN 15
1966 APR 15
JAN 25
1973 [illegible] 8

Cover page of the dossier of the Hungarian Secret Police, 1964

Translation[6]

Lines across the page:	Archives of the State Security Service
In the top left:	Listed details of the charge: He participated during the events of October in 1956 at the University of Szeged, in the preparation and distributions of counter-revolutionary tracts.
On the right:	Name and surname: Miklós Vető Place of birth: Budapest Date: 1936 Occupation: Student of law Completed studies: Secondary school diploma Address: Budapest, XIII. Sallai Street Citizenship: Hungarian Budapest, June 11, 1964 Signature of Mrs. Bela Toth, Lieutenant Checked by Mrs. (illegible), Colonel Deputy Director Dates of consultation between 1965 and 1978

6. After this page follows around fifty others containing confessions and accusations of the proceedings against the group of which Miklós Vető was a part, as well as pieces of information furnished by various informers of the Secret Police.

August 19, 1964

Dear Dr. Veto:

Please forgive me for my delay in answering your letter of July 29th. The end of the summer session made the past two weeks quite hectic for me. In addition, and more important, I have wanted to think about your letter before answering it.

I need hardly say, of course, that your letter raises a number of very important issues which have concerned me for some time. For this reason, I welcome this correspondence for it will enable both of us to put on paper and therefore crystallize our thoughts on some of these matters.

We have a common point of departure: our rejection of all anthropocentric theology. God cannot be spun out of human substance, even of the loftiest portion of it. We are therefore driven to the self-revelation of God as the source of our theology and this leads us to scripture. Now it is of course true that for the Christian scripture means the New Testament as well as the Old. But when the church, against the objections of people such as Marcion, irrevocably felt itself drawn also under the authority of the Hebrew Bible, a faith event of such magnitude took place that only today can we begin to assess the full significance of it. For the present, I will speak of only one dimension of this matter: the election of Israel. It is a fundamental claim of the Hebrew Bible that of all the peoples and nations of the world, God selected Abraham and his seed for his own. From the point of view of reason this naturally is an absurdity. Why should the the Lord of Creation be partial to one individual and one nation? But it seems incontrovertible that the God of Abraham, Isaac and Jacob took this "stiff necked" and "rebellious" people (Deut. IX:6) and tied the redemption of man to its fate. "For thou art a holy people unto the Lord thy God, and the Lord has chosen thee to be His own treasure out of all peoples that are upon the face of the earth." (Deut. XIV: 2) Not that Israel was ever worthy of this election! While the history of this people has consisted, as Barth points out, of a perpetual rebellion against the grace of God, there has nevertheless always remained a remnant faithful to the covenant and to the God of their fathers. And in witness of its election, this people has undegone the crucifixion of history, the most terrible chapter of which our own generation has witnessed. The passion of Jesus is continuous with the passion of his people into whose suffering he merged his own. To be a Jew, therefore, is to carry in one's flesh God's election, his never ending faithfulness and the ever present call to crucifixion that is the mark of election.

Now I would argue that even from a devoutly Christian point of view, this election of the seed of Abraham is irrevocable. I am aware that much of traditional Christian thought considers the election of the old Israel to be superceded by that of the new Israel, the community of those faithful to Christ. As you point out, Balthasar does not accept this, nor does Barth. Why? Because to do so one must spiritualize the OT, read it with a turn away from the concrete, specific and historical toward the universal and inner, a reading more appropriate to the gnostic than the Christian. The OT is not a book of secrets; its prophets do not speak in riddles to be understood only by the initiated. Here I hope you will forgive me for saying this, but much of past Christian exegesis of the OT, in reading it as prefiguration of the New, introduces a hermeneutic method that pits the inner against the outer, the spiritual against the material. When this method, in turn, is applied to the New Testament, we get Christian gnosis or some sort of Hegeliansim. The God of Abraham, Isaac and Jacob is not a God of secret spiritual meanings whose dignity is impaired by the realities of human history in the fullness of the material dimension that is human nature. The election of the seed of Abraham is not the election of the members of a philosophic school or of a mystery cult of those with secret gnosis. It is the election of a family, of people related in blood whose physiognomy is recognizable to the God-hating carricaturists of Der Sturmer. Such a people God has elected and instead of degrading it, it glorifies him in his faithfulness to this people and through it of all peoples in their particularity and the fullness of their particular humanity.

I am eager to hear your reaction to what I have said. I have not answered your question concerning my view of philosophy. I will write about that later.

Thank you very much for sending your dissertation. I am in the midst of reading it. Edith sends her regards.

Cordially,

Michael W.

Letter from Michael Wyschogrod, August 1964[7]

7. [This note combines four notes in the original French edition.] K. Barth (1886–1968) was the greatest Christian theologian of the 20th century. H. Urs von Balthasar (1905–1988) was the greatest Catholic theologian of the 20th century. [Der Stürmer was a] Nazi publication. Michael Wyschogrod (1928–2015) was an American Jewish theologian and philosopher.

Jerusalem, November 27, 1964

Dear Dr. Vető,

I received your letter of November 7 concerning Schelling and Molitor. My answers can be very simple. As to Schelling, you want to have a fuller documentation on the subject of Schelling's interest in Cabbalism and his knowledge on this topic. You are apparently unaware, that there is a special publication on this subject, namely Wilhelm August Schulze: Schelling und die Kabbala, published in the Swiss Quarterly JUDAICA, Beitraege zum Verstaendnis des juedischen Schicksals, Zuerich, Zwingli Verlag, 13. Jahrgang, Heft 2-4, Juni-Dezember, 1957. It is evident, that if you wish to write on Schelling's doctrine of creation in his later philosophy you will have to be well acquainted with the work of both Oetinger and Franz Baader, who made a deep impact on Schelling, although he always tried to hide it and never admitted it openly. I am not conversant with the literature on the later Schelling which is mushrooming in our time, but I am sure that many of these books and articles touch on the topic of your dissertation. Schelling's knowledge of things Cabbalistic is of course indirect and not based on any serious study of genuine Cabbalistical sources.

As to Molitor, who was a great admirer of Baader, there is no point in writing about him without the knowledge of Hebrew. I am sorry but I can only confirm your pessimism regarding this question.

Together with your letter I received the volume "Auf gespaltenem Pfad", Festschrift fuer Margarete Susman, Zum 90. Geburtstag, herausgegeben von Manfred Schloesser, Erato Presse, Darmstadt, 1964. This volume contains on pages 186-215 an article by Hugo Bergman (Jerusalem): "Schelling kommentiert die Genesis", which directly concerns the subject matter of your dissertation.

Yours sincerely,

G. Scholem

Letter from Gershon Scholem, November 27, 1964[8]

8. [This note combines five notes in the original French edition.] Schelling (1775–1854), a philosopher, was one of the great representatives of German idealism. F. Molitor (1779–1860) was a German philosopher and the author of important works on Jewish mysticism. Kabbalah is one of the most important manifestations of Jewish speculative mysticism from the Middles Ages until the 17th century. F. C. Oetinger (1702–1782) was a German theologian. F. Baader (1765–1841) was a German philosopher. G. Scholem (1897–1982) is the most celebrated authority and historian of Kabbalah.

CENTRE RICHELIEU
ÉTUDIANTS CATHOLIQUES DE SORBONNE
8, PLACE DE LA SORBONNE - PARIS Ve
ADRESSE TÉLÉGRAPHIQUE : CENTRICHELIEU-PARIS
ODE. 36-90 C. C. P. 7639-89

Paris,
le 2 janvier 1966

Chers amis,

Vous ne pouvez savoir combien votre mot m'a causé de joie.

Oui ! un certain type d'amitié supporte d'autant mieux la distance qu'il se situe dans la liberté la plus élective c'est à dire en Dieu. Et elle permet au coeur et à la chair de tressaillir de joie. Mon « centuple dès cette terre » (« avec des persécutions ») ce sont quelques rares amis comme vous.

Dieu vous bénisse tous trois et vous garde dans sa paix et sa joie.

Un rapprochement, pourtant, fait que vous pouvez peut-être utilement me renseigner.

Letter from Jean-Marie Lustiger (1926–2007), Cardinal Archbishop of Paris, 1966

Sur la recommandation et l'invitation du Pr RUHLMANN (prof de chinois aux Langues'O – fort original sur les bords) ~~mon~~ le Centre propose au

Rd William Sloane COFFIN

Aumônier des étudiants protestants de YALE de faire une conférence au Centre le 18 ou 19 janvier 1966 sur

les Universitaires américains et la guerre au Viet Nam.

Avez-vous une opinion sur le Rd ou sur son sujet ? Si oui, et si elle est négative ou restrictive, écrivez-moi *vite* par retour du courrier. Sinon, écrivez quand même mais lorsque vous en avez le temps.

Amitié

[illegible]

Translation

Dear Friends,

You cannot know how much joy your note has given me.

Yes! A certain type of friendship bears all the better the distance that is situated in the most elective freedom, that is to say, in God. And it permits the heart and the flesh to rejoice. That which is "even now my hundredfold" ("with persecutions") is the few rare friends like you.

God bless the three of you and keep you in His peace and His joy.

A fortuitous reconnection makes it possible for you to perhaps helpfully provide some information for me.

On the recommendation and invitation of Professor RUHLMANN (professor of Chinese in the School of Oriental Languages—he is very original by the way), the Center proposes to the Reverend William Sloan COFFIN, chaplain of the Protestant students of Yale to hold a lecture at the Richelieu Center on January 18 or 19, 1966, on the American universities and the Vietnam War.

Have you an opinion on the Reverend or about his subject? If so, and if it is negative or restrictive, write to me *quickly* by return mail. If not, write anyway, but when you have the time for it.

In friendship,
J. M. Lustiger
Paris
January 2, 1966

NANTERRE, LE 23 janvier 1967

UNIVERSITÉ DE PARIS

FACULTÉ DES LETTRES ET SCIENCES HUMAINES

AVENUE DE LA RÉPUBLIQUE
92 - NANTERRE

TÉL. : 204-34-32
204-29-87 à 91
204-39-87 à 91

Département de Philosophie

Cher Ami ,

Je vous renvoie votre texte sur la Facticité et l'ambiguïté de Dieu selon Schelling. Je ne m'en rappelle plus si je vous en avais parlé à Yale ? Une seule chose m'inquiète: votre modernisation du langage de Schelling . Il n'est plus guère éclairant aujourd'hui de présenter Schelling comme un précurseur de l'existentialisme , d'autant que ce mot est devenu très équivoque, depuis qu'il est pratiquement capté par la première philosophie de Sartre. Ce que vous dites de Schelling lui-même se suffit parfaitement. Il est peut-être beaucoup plus important de replacer ces recherches dans la perspective d'une théologie du Dieu vivant , opposée au monothéisme abstrait de la philosophie pré-kantienne et kantienne . Ce qui me frappe de plus en plus chez Schelling, et aussi chez Hegel, c'est la volonté de prendre au sérieux la question d'une vie propre de

Letter from the philosopher Paul Ricœur (1913–2005), January 1967

Dieu , support d'un vie ad extra; que que soit le péril de la théosophie, c'est la fonction irremplaçable de l'idéalisme allemand d'avoir osé mettre le mouvement , l'obscurité et la passion en Dieu . Mais Platon l'avait deviné, lorsqu'il écrivait dans Le Sophiste : "Eh ! quoi par Zeus , nous laisserons-nous si facilement convaincre que le mouvement , la vie , l'âme , la pensée n'ont réellement point de place au sein de l'être universel, qu'il ne vit ni ne pense et que , solennel et sacré, vide d'intellect, Il reste là planté sans bouger? - l'effrayante doctrine que nous accepterions là, étranger". (Sophiste , 249 a).

Je vous remercie d'avoir gardé les objets oubliés dans mon appartement . Si vous voulez bien , je vous les laisse jusqu'à l'automne prochain.

D'autre part la bibliothèque universitaire me demande de lui adresser la dissertation de John K. Roth sur Willaim James . Je pense l'avoir laissée dans la salle de séjour de mon appartement . Auriez-vous l'obligeance de venir l'y prendre et de la remettre à Mrs. Loretta C Monahan, assistant Registrar.

Recevez , cher Miklos Vetö, mes bien cordiales pensées et partagez avec votre femme mes vœux pour votre foyer, votre enseignement et votre œuvre

P.Ricoeur

Amicalement

P. Ricoeur

Translation

Dear Friend,

I return your text on the facticity and ambiguity of God according to Schelling. I no longer remember if I had spoken to you at Yale? Only a single thing troubles me: your modernization of the language of Schelling. It is hardly any longer illuminating today to present Schelling as a precursor to existentialism, especially because this word has become quite equivocal, being [now] practically captured by the first philosophy of Sartre. That which you say of Schelling himself is perfectly sufficient. It is perhaps much more important to reposition these findings in the perspective of a theology of the living God, as opposed to the abstract monotheism of pre-Kantian and Kantian philosophy. That which strikes me more and more in Schelling, and also in Hegel, is the desire to take seriously the question of a life proper to God, support of a life *ad extra*; whatever be the peril of the theosophy, it is the irreplaceable function of German idealism to have dared to put movement, obscurity, and passion into God. But Plato had guessed it, as he wrote in the *Sophist*: "But for heaven's sake, are we going to be convinced that it's true that change, life, soul, and intelligence are not present in *that which wholly is*, and that it neither lives nor thinks, but stays changeless, solemn, and holy, without any understanding? [. . .] If we did, sir, we'd be admitting something frightening" (*Sophist*, 249a).

I thank you for having kept the forgotten objects in my apartment. If you would like, I will leave them with you until next autumn.

On the other hand, the university library is asking me to send it the dissertation of John K. Roth on William James. I think I've left it in the living room of my apartment. Would you be kind enough to go take it and deliver it to Mrs. Loretta C. Monahan, the assistant registrar?

Receive, dear Miklós Vető, my cordial wishes, and share with your wife my wishes for your home, your teaching, and your work.

Amicably,

P. Ricœur

January 23, 1967

Fled Hungary

Veto Recalls Revolution

By WILLIAM HENRY

"I remember on the day of the Revolution - October 23, 1956 - I made a speech, exhorting my fellow students not to march that night in protest. Then, that evening, I found myself totally taken up, completely involved in the crowd."

Thus, with a burst of youthful impulsiveness, 20-year-old Miklos Veto joined the uprising that was to become the Hungarian Revolution.

Within four months, he would find himself wandering across Yugoslavia, reaching a refugee camp, and beginning a new life that would send him to Paris, London, and the American Midwest before he would settle in suburban Hamden as a teacher of philosophy at Yale.

"I was not involved in the Revolution in the sense that I was fighting with arms," Veto says. "Yes, I had a few hand grenades at home. But in the city I was in, there was no fighting."

Yet Veto played an active enough role in "subversive activities" to be put on trial twice. Both charges were dismissed, once because it was thought Veto had already escaped, the second time because he actually had fled to Yugoslavia.

Veto is reluctant to speak in detail about his part in the Revolution, for he hopes one day to return to Hungary. "It is unlikely that there would be any trouble," he explains in a lilting accent that reveals his years at the Sorbonne as well as his youth in Budapest.

"But if there were any problems, I would be in a great deal of trouble. You see, I have no nationality."

Secret Police

Yet, despite his fears about discussing his involvement in the insurrection, Veto has a number of stories to tell. "The greatest physical harm I faced," he says, "was on that first evening. I got a flying kick and went flying myself.

"I was kicked by a secret policeman — one of those fat, thick, square men in plain clothes — and I was a lean young boy at the time. I landed several feet away, and I must confess I did not go back to hit him."

After that, the dangers facing Veto were more legal than physical. Once he was stopped on the street while carrying a briefcase full of speeches, leaflets and other antigovernment propaganda. "I must have been held for only a few minutes, I suppose," he remembers, "but I was sure it was at least half an hour."

Although he faced sure imprisonment if discovered, Veto managed to stay cool. He convinced the policeman that the bag contained only lecture notes. "But I was so frightened," Veto says, "I went home and I burned everything in that bag."

The same coolness under pressure saved Veto as he headed for the Yugoslavian border in early 1957. Three times in five days he was stopped by border guards.

"They arrested most of the people on my train," Veto recalls. "We were all questioned for minor things, because we were near the border. And they took most of us away."

'Keeping a Good Attitude'

But Veto "kept a good attitude," so much so that at the end of one search the investigating officer apologized for having disturbed him.

"Things were particularly tense by the time I left," he says. "The Austrian border was completely sealed off, and the Yugoslavian border was very, very tight." Of 119,000 refugees, Veto was among the last 800 to leave the country. "I felt a sense of duty to stay in Hungary as long as I could," he says. Thus, the first time he was to go on trial, he hid for two days rather than flee. The court assumed he had already escaped, and dropped the charges.

Veto stayed for another six weeks. During that time he wrote an open letter to the Prime Minister, criticizing the government, and again he was a wanted man.

MIKLOS VETO

"We were the last organization going. Right up to the end, we had a mimeograph machine producing pamphlets and posters. When the government heard that we had a mimeograph, they came to destroy it. But we were ready."

A contact within the secret police, Veto recalls, tipped off the revolutionaries that investigators were on their way. The mimeograph had long been converted to the shape of a clothes iron. So, when the police arrived they found only a group of students talking -- and several freshly ironed shirts. "They did not bother to check the iron," Veto says.

Time to Flee

Shortly after that, a series of incidents convinced Veto that the time had come for him to flee. A girl member of the movement was arrested along with her father, who suffered from heart disease. When questioned, the girl would reveal nothing.

Then, Veto narrates, the police began to beat the father while the girl watched, and she talked.

Released after her confession, the girl joined another young woman, and the second girl's fiance, in an attempt to escape. "They later found out they had been in Yugoslavia," Veto says, "but they wandered around some more.

"After two days, they were so thirsty that they stopped at a house for a drink. It was the Hungarian secret police, and they were arrested."

At last Veto began the treacherous journey across the border. After several harrowing searches, he made it to Yugoslavia, where he wound up in a refugee camp.

"The man who brought us across the border," he recalls, was a spy for the Russians, the Yugoslavians, and formerly the Germans. The Yugoslavians became suspicious, and wanted me to testify against him. I would not, so they sent me to the worst refugee camp."

Penniless In France

After three months in Yugoslavia, Veto went to Paris to study at the Sorbonne. He was almost penniless, but the French government charges nominal tuition, and they provided housing, clothing, and other aid.

"They even sent me to the Alps and the Riviera on vacations," Veto says. "Once I decided to go to the Basque coast. When I decided that instead I would go all the way into Spain, they still gave me half the money I would have had for a stay in France."

Veto studied at the Sorbonne for three years, completing both bachelor's and master's degrees. (While in Hungary, he had been a junior at the University of Szeged.)

During 1959, while still officially enrolled at the Sorbonne, Veto left for London to learn English. At that point, he was already fluent in French, German, Latin, Russian and Hungarian.

While in England, Veto visited Oxford. There he met the noted philosopher Sir Isaiah Berlin, who took a liking to the plucky 23-year-old, and arranged for a full-expenses doctoral grant for Veto.

Veto "could not turn down such an offer," and set up residence in England in 1959, even before he had officially completed his master's from the Sorbonne.

In 1962, he married Odile Wattre, whom he had met at the Sorbonne's Catholic Students' Center. By fall of 1963, Veto was ready to leave Europe for the United States, although he would not be awarded his doctorate until 1964, in absentia.

He then came to Marquette University in Milwaukee, "the bottom of the earth. Once I was on an open housing march and the students at the university hung out their windows looking at us as though we were monkeys."

Veto and wife Odile taught at Marquette for two years, he in the philosophy department and she in French. Then, in 1965, Veto joined the Yale staff, and in 1966 Mrs. Veto was named to a Yale post. Currently they are assistant professors of philosophy and romance languages respectively.

Mrs. Veto is trilingual — her specialty is Italian, she is a native of France, and she is fluent in English. She knows a bit of Hungarian as well.

Son Etienne, 3, speaks fluent French and English, understands

(continued on page 5)

Veto Recalls Youth

(continued from page 3)

Spanish and a bit of German. Nicholas, three months, will be at least bilingual, for French is the language spoken in the Veto home

Perplexed On War

Veto takes an active interest in the political scene.

He admits to a perplexed duality about the Vietnam war, for example. "Four months ago, on a weekend retreat at a Carmelite monastery, I realized that tne war is wrong.

"It is immoral, and impractical. The United States cannot win. You just cannot militarily win a war like that. But I am an anti-Communist, and my guts tell me that Iwant the United States to win while my brain tells me that they should not."

On the question of student activism, Veto is firmly resolved. Of groups like S.D.S., he says, "They should do more." But American students, Veto claims, are ill-suited to activism.

Most of them, he notes, "are only slightly better off than everyone else. Only the very rich and the very poor can afford to be radical. Also, the students here are politically inarticulate. They do not know so well what is going on."

As for his own experiences as an activist, Veto has no regrets. "The Revolution made a man of me," he says. "I was very schoolish, very bookish, very clumsy about anything physical – I still cannot open a can.

"Then came the revolution, and for a fifteen-day period I felt fully free, I felt the pure, exhilarating, uncontrolled freedom—the absolute freedom—of knowing that everything you are doing is totally right."

It was not until the Revolution, he adds, that he "came to believe in the existence of evil."

Since then, his studies, his thesis, his magazine articles (printed in France, Belgium, Italy, Britain, the United States, and soon in Canada), and his two forthcoming books have focused on the philosophical implications of evil and suffering.

Willam Henry, Vető recalls youth, Yale Daily News, April 24, 1968

Mr Gabriel MARCEL
2I, rue de Tournon
PARIS VIème

Paris, le 26 Décembre 1968

Monsieur Nicolas Vetö
Department of Philosophy
YALE UNIVERSITY
NEW HAVEN - Connecticut

U.S.A.

Cher Nicolas Vetö,

Je vous remercie beaucoup de votre lettre : votre fidélité me touche profondément et j'avais eu bien grand plaisir à vous revoir à Vienne en Septembre. Depuis cette rencontre, j'ai fait une rapide et fatigante tournée de conférences en Espagne que j'abordais avec inquiétude et qui s'est déroulée dans de bonnes conditions. Je suis rentré très fatigué, mais vais bien maintenant, avec les handicaps habituels, naturellement auxquels on ne peut rien changer.

Je suis heureux des nouvelles que vous me donnez et de la décision que vous avez prise de passer l'an prochain en France. Quand vous serez naturalisé, il sera beaucoup plus facile pour vous de vous insérer dans l'Université Française. Je me demande par quel biais vous abordez Schelling : sujet redoutable entre tous , le Père Tilliette qui le travaille depuis quinze ans a bien failli s'y casser les reins ! Ses thèses sont terminées, ou presque maintenant, mais il demande comment il arrivera à les publier, vue leur énormité. Et une autre thèse sur Schelling est en préparation, celle de Marquet qui donne les plus grandes espérances. Mais je suppose que votre thèse,

-2-

la soutiendez aux U.S.A. ou bien, est-ce que je me trompe ?

Le drame du Biafra constitue un scandale sans nom et suffit à montrer que nous vivons dans un monde criminel. Ma belle soeur, avec qui j'habite, a risqué une allusion devant une amie anglaise que nous aimons beaucoup, et celle-ci a eu l'impudence de dire :"mais vous savez, on meurt aussi de faim de l'autre coté": ce qui est un mensonge.

Je connais très mal l'oeuvre de Barth, mais il se peut que vous ayez raison. C'est moi qui avais écrit le petit rapport introductif, lorsqu'il y a un an, nous avons élu Barth comme membre associé de l'Académie des Sciences Morales et Politiques.

Ai-je besoin de vous dire que le problème de l'Université n'est nullement résolu ici et que l'épidémie d'insubordination qui s'étend à beaucoup de lycées nous donne de très graves préoccupations. Ma petite fille qui a été reçue très brillamment à l'Agrégation de Philosophie en Septembre et qui est Professeur au Lycée du Havre (elle vient d'avoir 22 ans !) a elle-même beaucoup de difficultés.

Je vous adresse mes voeux les plus affectueux pour l'année qui vient et me réjouis de penser que je vous reverrai probablement tous deux dans quelques mois.

G. Marcel

Gabriel MARCEL
de l'Institut

Letter from Gabriel Marcel (1889–1973), Christian existentialist, December 1968

Translation

Dear Nicolas Vető,

I thank you greatly for your letter: your fidelity touches me profoundly, and I truly had great pleasure to see you again in Vienna during September. Since that meeting, I have made a rapid and tiring speaking tour in Spain, which I completed with some distress, but which unfolded under good conditions. I returned very fatigued, but am now well, albeit with habitual handicaps, for which one naturally cannot do anything to change.

I am happy about the news that you have given me and about the decision that you have taken to pass the next year in France. When you are naturalized, it will be much easier for you to insert yourself into the French university. I wonder by what means you approach Schelling. Being such a formidable subject, Father Tilliette, who has worked on him for fifteen years, almost broke his back over him. His theses are finished now, or almost so, but he wonders how he will manage to publish them, seeing their enormity. And another thesis on Schelling is in preparation, the one of Marquet, who gives the greatest hopes. But I suppose that your thesis will be defended in the United States, or is it that I am mistaken?

The tragedy of Biafra constitutes an unspeakable scandal and suffices to show that we live in a criminal world. My sister-in-law, with whom I live, had risked an allusion in front of an English friend whom we very much love, and she had the impudence to say, "but, you know, on the other hand, one also dies of hunger on the other side," which is a lie.

I only very poorly know the work of Barth, but it may be that you are right. It was I who wrote the small introductory report when, one year ago, we elected Barth as an associate of the Academy of Moral and Political Sciences.

Have I need to tell you that the problem of the University is in no manner resolved here, and that the epidemic of insubordination, which is spreading through many of the secondary schools, is giving us very serious preoccupations. My granddaughter who has been received quite brilliantly in the philosophy aggregation in September, and who is a teacher at Le Havre High School (she has just turned twenty-two!), has many difficulties herself.[9]

I send you my most affectionate wishes for the coming year and rejoice in thinking that I will probably see you both in a few months.

Gabriel Marcel
of the Institute
Paris
December 26, 1968

9. Aggregation is a competitive examination, and those received—about five percent—will have a job either in the final year of high school, or more and more frequently in higher education, that is, college or university.

THE INSTITUTE FOR ADVANCED STUDY
PRINCETON, NEW JERSEY 08540

SCHOOL OF MATHEMATICS

Le 12 octobre 1970.

Cher Monsieur,

Je m'excuse du retard apporté à vous répondre. Bien entendu vous avez mon autorisation pour les citations à insérer dans votre thèse. Je ne crois pas bien utile que vous m'en envoyiez un relevé; en revanche, je serais content d'avoir une copie de la bibliographie, mais je préférerais que vous m'adressiez cela à Paris après le 15 janvier, car je serai à Paris pour plusieurs mois à partir de cette date.

Naturellement je serai content aussi d'avoir un exemplaire de votre thèse quand elle sera imprimée.

Si vous avez l'occasion de venir à Princeton cet automne, ne manquez pas de me faire signe; j'aurai plaisir à vous revoir.

Bien cordialement à vous

A.Weil

Letter from André Weil (1906–1998), brother of Simone Weil, and one of the greatest mathematicians of the 20th century

Translation

Dear Sir,

I excuse myself for the tardiness taken in responding to you. Of course you have my authorization to insert the citations into your thesis. I do not believe it very useful to send me a list of these; on the other hand, I would be happy to have a copy of the bibliography, but I would prefer you send that to my address in Paris after January 15, because I will be in Paris for several months from that date onward.

Naturally, I will also be happy to have a copy of your thesis when it is printed.

If you have occasion to come to Princeton this autumn, do not fail to signal me; it will be my pleasure to receive you.

Very cordially,
A. Weil
October 12, 1970

Abidjan, le 10 Juin 1977

Monsieur VETO
Maître de Conférences de Philosophie
B.P. 2034

ABIDJAN

à Son Excellence Monsieur le Président Félix HOUPHOUET BOIGNY

Monsieur le Président,

Assistant technique français en Côte d'Ivoire depuis 1975, j'ai eu maintes occasions d'observer l'esprit humanitaire et tolérant qui inspire la vie publique de ce pays. On se sent en sécurité et en liberté et on constate le respect de l'homme, phénomène, hélas, de plus en plus restreint dans notre monde d'aujourd'hui. Dans ces conditions excellentes nous sommes particulièrement troublés par la situation qui prévaut au Commissariat de Police adjacent à la Mairie de Cocody. Nos fenêtres donnent sur la place du Marché et souvent au milieu de la nuit ou même en pleine journée nous entendons les cris et les hurlements des personnes maltraitées par certains policiers. Ils sont battus, souvent fouettés, leurs plaintes s'entendent bien loin et effrayent nos enfants.

Etant étranger je n'ai aucune velléité de formuler une critique quelconque à l'adresse des autorités ivoiriennes mais je me sens obligé de porter à votre très haute attention ces actes violents qui se perpétuent dans les locaux de la police de Cocody. Nous espérons qu'il s'agit de faits isolés mais il faut qu'ils soient portés à la connaissance de celui qui protège les droits de tous les habitants de ce pays.

J'ai pensé originellement vous remettre cette lettre à la sortie de la messe de l'ISCR où nous allons, nous aussi, mais j'ai préféré ne pas vous déranger le dimanche.

Je vous prie, Monsieur le Président, d'agréer l'expression de ma très Haute considération.

M. Veto

Mr. VETO

Letter to Félix Houphouët-Boigny (1905–1993), President of the Republic of the Ivory Coast (June 10, 1977)

Translation

To His Excellence, President Félix Houphouët-Boigny

Mister President,

As a French technical assistant in the Ivory Coast since 1975, I have had numerous occasions to observe the humanitarian and tolerant spirit that inspires the public life of this country. We feel safe and free, and we note the respect that one has for his fellow human beings—something, alas, more and more limited in our world of today. In these excellent conditions, we are particularly troubled by the situation that prevails in the police station adjacent to the Cocody city hall. Our windows open onto Market Square, and often in the middle of the night, or even in broad daylight, we hear the screams and cries of people mistreated by certain police officers. They are beaten, often flogged, and their groans are heard from afar, frightening our children.

Being a foreigner, I have no wish to formulate any criticism and address it to Ivorian authorities, but I feel myself obligated to bring to your very high attention these violent acts that are perpetrated on police premises in Cocody. We hope that this concerns isolated instances, but it is necessary that they be brought to the attention of he who protects the rights of all the inhabitants of this country.

I originally thought to hand you this letter upon exit from the Mass at the ICAO [*Institut Catholique d'Afrique Occidentale*] where we also go, but I preferred not to disturb you on a Sunday.

Please accept, Mister President, the expression of my highest consideration.

M. Vető

June 10, 1977

CH-4051 BASEL, DEN 19.1.86
ARNOLD BÖCKLINSTRASSE 42

Cher Monsieur,
votre lettre et votre introduction à G.G. me met dans un réel embarras. D'une part, votre présentation est passionnante (peut-être que l'insistance sur le néant au début est un peu trop lourde), d'autre part je ne puis risquer une anthologie dans ma petite maison d'édition, et il sera difficile de trouver un éditeur de textes (presqu')inconnus de l'avant-guerre. Il faudrait peut-être aborder quelques bons philosophes chrétiens: Robert Spaemann, Jörg Splett, Hommes, Oeing-Hanhoff.. Si l'un d'eux propose la publication à Herder ou à Grünewald, je verrais une chance. Je vois bien qu'avec cette proposition je double votre travail, et je m'en excuse. On pourrait même penser à Meiner ou à Klostermann comme éditeurs. Mais il faudrait pour cela un bon avocat.

Si vous faites ce choix de textes, il faudra bien choisir les thèses plus originales de l'auteur – quelques-unes sont un peu „de commun!"

Si je dois renvoyer le texte, faites-moi signe – sinon pas besoin de répondre.

Bien à vous et bon travail.

Hans Balthasar

Letter from Hans Urs von Balthasar (January, 1986)

Translation

Dear Sir,

Your letter and your introduction to Gondos-Grünhut put me in a real state of embarrassment. On the one hand, your presentation is fascinating (perhaps the insistence on nothingness at the beginning is a little too heavy-handed). On the other hand, I cannot risk an anthology in a small publishing house, and it will be difficult to find a publisher for (almost) unknown texts from the pre-war period. It would be necessary perhaps to approach some good Christian philosophers, Robert Spaemann, Jörg Splett, Hommes, Oeing-Hanhoff . . . If one among them were to propose the publication to Herder or Grünewald, I would see a chance. I see that with this proposition I trouble your work, and for this, I beg your pardon. One could even think of Meiner or Klostermann as publishers. But, for that, one would need a good advocate.

If you make this choice of texts, the most original theses of the author are to be chosen—some are a little "*de communi*."

If I must send back the text, let me know; if not, no need to respond.

Wishes for you and your work,

Hans Balthasar

January 19, 1986

١٧
AN-NAHAR Mercredi 12 Avril 2000

الباحث الفلسفي ميكلوس فيتو في حديث الى "النهار":

لا اختبار أقوى من اختبار العدم

"فلسفة الدين ومسالكها المعاصرة" علوان محوري دار حوله المؤتمر الذي نظمته كلية الآداب والعلوم الانسانية، فرع الفلسفة، في الذكرى الـ١٢٥ لتأسيس جامعة القديس يوسف، في اشراف عميدها الاب اليسوعي رينيه شاموسي وتنظيم المسؤولة عن فرع الفلسفة السيدة نيكول حاتم. اساتذة في الفلسفة ومفكرون من جامعات فرنسا دعتهم الجامعة لمناقشة هذا الموضوع المقلق، المثير، مزودين مراجع متشعبة من فكر نيتشه وهايدغر وفيبر "وباسكال وسواهم من الفلاسفة الذين تطرقوا الى فلسفة الدين، وبينهم جان ميشال لونيو من جامعة نامور، وميكلوس فيتو من جامعة بواتييه، وناتالي ديبراز من جامعة باريس، وجان غريش من المعهد الكاثوليكي في باريس، وجاد حاتم ونيكول حاتم من جامعة القديس يوسف. على ضوء فكر الفيلسوف المعاصر لازلو غوندوش غرونهوت قدم ميكلوس فيتو Veto الاستاذ في جامعة بواتييه محاضرته. والفكر الاكاديمي الذي يتحلى به فيتو، بسطه وانسنه في حديث شائق الى "النهار" منبثقا من رؤى غوندوش غرونهوت.

ميكلوس فيتو، الرحلة عن العدم إلى الله.

• هلاّ عرّفتنا بلازلو غوندوش غرونهوت.

– إنه فيلسوف هنغاري توفي عام ١٩٦١ عن ثمانية وخمسين عاما، تاركا مؤلفات عدة باللغتين الالمانية والهنغارية، جوهرها الميتافيزيكية الصوفية. والحدس الجوهري لفكره يدور حول العدم، ومن فكره هذا ان الله قاهر العدم ومانح الخليقة قوة السيطرة عليه. ووسعت محاضرتي انطلاقا من جدلية العلاقات بين الله والعدم والانسان. انها جدلية قائمة على المجانية والمحبة.

• بين اهم مؤلفاتك "الماورائية الدينية لدى سيمون فيل" و"الاساس لدى شيلنغ" و"فكر جوناثان إدواردز" ومن "كانط الى شيلنغ" في مسلكي المثال الالماني، لماذا اخترت غوندوش غرونهوت من بين جميع هؤلاء لمحاضرتك؟

– لعل خياري هذا نبع من إرادة شخصية ترسم قدر مساري. ترعرعت في بلد شيوعي. كنت ملحدا حتى الثامنة عشرة، ثم

رحمة ولا رجاء. ساحة رعب وعنف وقسوة.

• وهل من خيارات وضعت امام الانسان لصد هذا الواقع؟

– اما ان نتصرف مع هذا العالم كأنه الحقيقة الوحيدة المطابقة للواقع، أو نستمر في إيماننا بالخير

اسلوب تصويري المسائل التقليدية المتعلقة بما وراء الطبيعة، لكنه لم يقصر اهتمامه على المستلزمات التقنية للفلسفة. مشروعه الحقيقي ديني، ولم يتوزع بين المفاهيم الدينية والمفاهيم الفلسفية. اعتبرهما وكأنهما الحدثان المهمان للمعرفة الحقيقية.

• كيف اضاء هذه المعرفة؟

– كتب يقول ان هذه المعرفة هي الميتافيزيكا المكونة من الاونطولوجيا Ontologie اي علم الكائن، والعلم الروحاني. قال ان الاونطولوجيا هي العلم العقلاني المتفوق، بينما يترجم العلم الروحاني تجربة الغبطة التي تهبها الحياة مع الله.

• وكأننا نعود بهذه العبارة الى بدايات حديثنا: الله قاهر العدم.

– بل اكثر. انه الانسان المسكون بالله الذي يستطيع ان يقهر ليل العدم. لكن الانسان ليس ثقة بحد ذاتها ولا يحرك دوما ان تقديره السامي لذاته لا يتحقق الا في

وحين كنت طالبا جامعيا كنا نتحلق ورفاقي حول فلاسفة روحانيين ونتشرب من فكرهم. لازلو غوندوش غرونهوت كان وحيي. مفكر روحي وضع مؤلفات عدة في المانيا إبان الثورة الهنغارية. وأدين لما أورثني اياه من رؤى فلسفية نبيلة، رائعة، منسية اليوم من البعض ويحفظها في اخلاص مفكرون ادركوا عمق بحثه وتمثلوا به. وذاك الدين الذي شعرت به واجبا حاولت تسديده في انطولوجيا جمعت فيها نصوص غوندوش الجوهرية مع مقدمة تعرف به واحسبها ضوءا على فكره نشرناها في مجلة متخصصة في تولوز. وها انا في هذا المؤتمر اواصل وفائي لفكره ويقيني انه يستحق أن يترجم في المحافل الفلسفية الدولية عوض ان يركن منسيا في محفوظات المكتبات. انها الارضية التي انطلقت منها عبر مشاركتي في هذا المؤتمر المتمحور حول "فلسفة الدين ومسالكها المعاصرة".

تجارب روحانية

● كيف تفسر نظرته العميقة في الله قاهر العدم؟

– هذا الرجل الملحد عاش تجربة روحانية صاعقة استخلص منها ان الانسان محاط بالعدم ومهدد منه، وان الكائن ليس حقيقة، وان الحياة ليست بينة، وأن المعنى ليس جليا. وكل تلك المفاهيم ينبغي ان تسلخ من عدم الوجود رغم تهديد العدم لها. فسلطان الخالق الفائق، المتجاوز للمستحيلات، وحده القادر على سلخ الانسان من العدم، وتحريره لا في شكل قاطع ونهائي، فوجود الله في الزمن البشري لا يتجلى الا من خلال صراع متواصل ضد قوى الجهل والشيطان. الله يعمل بلا توقف للتخفيف عن النفوس وعلينا نحن مساعدته.

الا يقول غوندوش غرونهوت انه من النبل والمنطقي ان يحارب كل بذاته الى جانب الله بدلا من ان نتوارى، مجهولين في تهيئة كمال ذاتي جماعي بعيد المدى؟

● كان الارض حيث نعيش مرصودة لصراع الانسان ضد عدمه؟

– انطلاقا من هذه المفاهيم ندرك ان ثمة فلسفة للتاريخ، غير مرتبطة بحقبات ومراحل، بل تشير امكانات الانسان وتصرفاته خارج عنصر الزمن. الانسان البدائي عاش في الجنة واكتسب حدسا يدله على محبة الله، فوجد العالم الذي يحوطه حكاية جميلة من الله. بيد ان هذه الرؤيا كتب لها أن تنكسر امام واقع الخير والشر. عالمنا منذ ذلك الحين تحول الى ساحة نزاعات بلا

[illegible] ما وراء هذا العالم [illegible]. الخيار الاول مصدره الالحاد، والثاني الاديان السماوية. الوثنية سلمت بهذا العالم الناقص، المسيء، واعتبرت قيمه قابلة للادراك. اما القوي والمنتصر فهو الذي ينجح في بسط نظرته للحق. امام هذه الرؤيا يبدو الله محدودا، غير كامل، وتختلف نظرة العالم اليه، ظالما او ضعيفا أو انه عجز هذا العالم بعدما شعر بعدم تأثيره عليه. أما الاديان السماوية فإيمانها كبير بالله الرحوم، المحب، رغم تجارب الارض المؤلمة. إنه الحقيقة المطلقة.

المشروع الديني

● كيف تمت رؤيا غوندوش غرونهوت الفلسفية؟

– اطلت خلال حقبة عالية من عالم الظاهرات. كان على علاقة بهوسرل وكان يعتبر كتابه الثاني "إيروس وأغابي" على انه المناقشة مع علم الكائن لدى هايدغر. منذ اطلالته راح يخاطب فلاسفة الماضي الاقدمين من افلاطون الى كانط، ثم اضاف اليهم برغسون.

غوندوش رجل فكر حلل في

[illegible]

الحقيقي الذي يسمو بالانسان فوق طبيعته الاصلية. تلك الحقيقة هي الله.

● ما هو الاختبار الاقسى الذي على الانسان ان يمر به للتفوق على طبيعته؟

– لا اختبار اقوى من اختبار العدم. هذا الضلال فوق الهوة السحيقة حافز لتذوق الفرح الحقيقي بالله. صراعنا في وجه العدم هو الاختبار الحقيقي الذي يوصلنا الى الفرح. فلولا هذا الاختبار لكان العالم مسطحا، مملاً تطفو على وجهه كائنات كئيبة، رخوة، عاجزة عن الاندهاش والامتنان.

● بين الوجود وعدمه كيف تطلو المشهد؟

– يقول غوندوش غرونهوت في ختام أطروحته: أمام علاقة الاشياء بالعدم وغياب واقعيتها ثمة شيء مناهض لعدم الوجود المحتوم، يريح من عبئه الثقيل. انه القدرة اللامتناهية التي تحوط بالاشياء والكائنات كي لا تغرق في العدم. تلك القدرة هي الوجود.

مي منسى

وطنٌ خلف المرايا

أينعتَ من ألف صبحٍ فوق أضرحتي   ماءً وعُشباً لِفتاكِ الوردِ والغزلِ
ترعى طفولةَ أحلامي وتنشرُها   فوقَ الرموشِ تراتيلاً لها شغلِ
ما كان قبلكَ محزونٌ تعهّدني   ولا ارتوى الماءَ مسّاً به أملِ
تلوحُ تبحرُ في عينيَّ متّشحاً   بعضَ المنى إذْ أنا أبكي وأنفعلُ

●

حاطتكَ من كلِّ وجهٍ ألفُ سنبلةٍ   حبلى يرتّلها الوجدانُ والمقلُ
لا وجهَ غيركَ للأرضِ التي انبجست   منها عيوني وفاضَ النبضُ والوجلُ
ما زلتَ أنتَ.. كأنتَ.. الآن في حرقي   أمسي إليكَ على حقلي أبتهلُ
واقتفيني.. وظلّي فوقَ أشرعتي   صبحٌ جنوبيّةٌ عيناهُ يحتفلُ

●

دوني المواسمُ أجلوها.. تورّطني   فيكَ النهاياتُ.. يمشي فوقنا الأزلُ
أنّي أفيقُ على جرحي تهدهدني   بداكَ موسمُ عطرٍ.. كفّهُ عسلُ
التاجُ والعمرُ مشدودٌ إلى قدمي   ولستُ أسألُ عمّن قبلنا أفلوا
ولستُ أسألُ هل غناكَ مؤتلقٌ   بعدي بنورك.. يا نوراً له قبلُ

●

يا صرحَ كلِّ جروحي أنتَ لي وطنٌ   خلفَ المرايا بحرُ الرملِ يغتسلُ
أهفو إلى الشمسِ في عينيكَ أقرأها   كالعهدِ تملأُ أعراسي وتنفصلُ
مالتْ تلوّحُ.. لم أسرجْ لها الّتي   ولم أطقْ أن يني إشعاعُها أجلُ
أيُّ المواجعِ أشهى بعدما انكسرتْ   عيناي فيها.. وضاقتْ بيننا السُّبلُ؟!

ياسين بن عبيد
الجزائر

Interview, An Nahar, Beirut (April 12, 2000)

Translation

The Philosopher, Miklós Vető, Confides in *Nahar*[10]

"There is no experience more powerful than the experience of nothingness."

"Philosophy of Religion and Its Contemporary Paths" is the title of a conference that was organized by the School of Letters and Human Sciences, Department of Philosophy, in memory of the one hundred and thirty years of Saint Joseph's University, [celebrated] under the patronage of its dean, Jesuit Father René Chamoussi, and the manager of the philosophy department, Mrs. Nicole Hatem, [herself a] professor of philosophy, and with the presence of the philosophy professors and thinkers from French universities, invited with a view to discuss this subject—reflecting upon the thought of Nietzsche, Heidegger, Pascal, and other philosophers of religion—among whom one can cite Jean-Michel Lanion from Nemours University, Miklós Vető from the University of Poitiers, Nathalie Depraz from the University of Paris, and Jean Greisch from the Catholic Institute of Paris, as well as Jad Hatem and Nicole Hatem from Saint Joseph's University. The lecture by Miklós Vető focused on the contemporary philosopher L. Gondos-Grünhut. The academic opinion of Vető, delivered in an interview by Nahar, commences with the vision of Gondos-Grünhut.

Nahar: Can you help us come to know Gondos-Grünhut?

Vető: He is a Hungarian philosopher who died in 1961, aged 59, leaving behind numerous works in German and Hungarian that essentially focus upon the metaphysics of spirituality. The essence of his thought revolves around nothingness, maintaining that God produces nothingness while nonetheless providing the creature with the capacity to master (dominate) it. I have developed my lecture based on the dialectic relation uniting God, nothingness, and man. It is a dialectic founded upon gratuity and love.

Nahar: Among your most important publications, one can cite *The Religious Metaphysics of Simone Weil*, *Le Fondement selon Schelling* (*The Ground According to Schelling*), *The Thought of Jonathan Edwards*, and *De Kant à Schelling. Les deux voies de l'Idéalisme allemande* (*From Kant to Schelling: The Two Paths of German Idealism*). Why have you chosen for your lecture

10. These pages are translated after the French translation by I. Fattal, University of Grenoble.

Gondos-Grünhut [rather than one from] among the ensemble of these [other] authors?

Vető: My choice originates from a personal will that represents the becoming of my life. I was raised in a communist country. I was heterodox/heretical until the age of eighteen, then I converted to the Catholic religion. And while I was a student at university, we gathered in circles, my friends and I, around philosophers of "the spirit," and we immersed ourselves in their thought. L. Gondos-Grünhut was an inspiration, a philosopher of the spirit himself who had produced works in German well before the Hungarian revolution. The revelation took place when I took notice of his sublime philosophical theories of religion, forgotten today by many, but conserved with devotion by thinkers who have understood the profundity of his thought and have identified themselves with him. And this engagement, which I have felt to be a duty, I have tried to realize in an anthology—gathering the essential texts of Gondos-Grünhut, with an introduction to make them known and meant to cast a light upon his thought.[11] Through my presence at this conference, I express my gratitude for his thought and my personal conviction that he merits to be translated instead of remaining forgotten in library reserves. Such is the reason for my participation in this conference, which centers on "the philosophy of religion and its contemporary paths."

11. See p. 39, n. 3.

Monsieur le Professeur
Miklos Vetö
50, rue Corvisart
F – 75013 Paris
France

Torny, le 3 octobre 2013

Monsieur le Professeur,

Votre lettre du 21 septembre m'est bien parvenue via mon fils Johannes et je vous en remercie très sincèrement.

Je ne m'occupe plus pour le moment de la canonisation du Roi Charles, mais je vais faire parvenir votre lettre au postulateur, afin qu'il en prenne connaissance.

Comme vous l'avez constaté lors de mes petites conférences, je mets toujours beaucoup l'accent sur le rôle de mon grand-père en Hongrie et, tout particulièrement, sur le très beau serment qu'il a fait lors de son couronnement. Ce serment explique bien une partie de son cheminement vers la Sainteté, ainsi que ses deux tentatives de restauration en Hongrie.

Je vous remercie d'avoir attiré mon attention au sujet que vous évoquez et vous prie de croire, Monsieur le Professeur, à l'expression de mes sentiments distingués et les meilleurs.

Prince R. de Hongrie.

Prince Rudolf de Hongrie

CHATEAU DE TORNY
CASE POSTALE 53
CH – 1746 PREZ-VERS-NOREAZ
SUISSE

Letter from Archduke Rudolf of Habsburg (2013)

Translation

Professor,

Your letter of September 21 has indeed reached me via my son Johannes, and for it, I very sincerely thank you.

I am, for the moment, no longer occupying myself with the canonization of King Charles, but I will have your letter reach the postulator, in order that he take notice of it.

As you noted during my small lectures, I have always put much stress on the role of my grandfather in Hungary, and particularly on the very beautiful oath he made during his coronation. This oath well explains part of his path toward holiness, as well as his two attempts of restoration in Hungary.

I thank you for having drawn my attention to the subject that you evoke, and I ask that you believe, Professor, in the expression of my distinguished and best sentiments.

Prince Rudolf of Hungary

October 3, 2013

Bibliography

Baranyai, Béla. "Nemzetközi Konferenciával Köszöntik a 80 Éves Vető Miklóst." Magyar Kurír, http://www.magyarkurir.hu/hirek/nemzetkozi-konferenciaval-koszontik-80-eves-veto-miklost/.

Baudelaire, Charles. *The Flowers of Evil.* Translated by James McGowan. New York: Oxford University Press, 1993.

Gondos-Grünhut, László. *Die Liebe Und Das Sein. Ein Auswahl.* Abhandlungen Zur Philosophie, Psychologie Und Pädagogik. Bonn: Bouvier, 1990.

Henry, William. "Veto Recalls Revolution (in 'Fled Hungary')." *The Yale Daily News,* April 24, 1968, 2–3.

Kant, Immanuel. *Critique of Pure Reason.* Translated by Paul Guyer and Allen W. Wood. The Cambridge Edition of the Works of Immanuel Kant. Edited by Paul Guyer and Allen W. Wood. New York: Cambridge University Press, 2009.

Lévi-Strauss, Claude. *Tristes Tropiques.* Translated by John Russell. New York: Criterion, 1961.

Lóránt, Czigány. *Ahol Állok, Ahol Megyek.* Budapest: Kortárs, 1998.

Madách, Imre. *The Tragedy of Man: Dramatic Poem.* Translated by William N. Loew. New York: Arcadia, 1908.

Pascal, Blaise. *Pensées and Other Writings.* Translated by Honor Levi. New York: Oxford University Press, 2008.

Veto, Miklos. *The Expansion of Metaphysics.* Translated by William C. Hackett. Eugene: Wipf and Stock, 2018.

———. *Le Fondement Selon Schelling.* 2nd ed., Paris: Harmattan, 2002.

———. *Gabriel Marcel. Les Grands Thèmes De Sa Philosophie.* Paris: Harmattan, 2014.

———. *De Kant À Schelling. Les Deux Voies De L'idéalisme Allemand.* 2 vols. Grenoble: Jérôme Millon, 1998–2000.

———. *The Religious Metaphysics of Simone Weil.* Translated by Joan Dargan. Alban, NY: The State University of New York Press, 1994.

———. *The Thought of Jonathan Edwards.* Translated by Philip Choinière-Shields. Edited by Rajat Acharya. Eugene: Wipf and Stock, in Press.

———. *De Whitehead À Marion. Éclats De Philosophie Contemporaine.* Paris: Harmattan, 2015.

Veto, Miklos, and Losoncz, Márk. "A Gyógyulást Az Jelentette, Amikor Az Álom Elmaradt. . ." *Híd* 9 (2015) 146–56.

www.ingramcontent.com/pod-product-compliance
Lightning Source LLC
Chambersburg PA
CBHW051110160426
43193CB00010B/1383
9781532668227